P9-DWS-255

URBAN
CYCLING

CALGARY PUBLIC LIBRARY

NOV   2016

– TO IRÈNE AND MAURICE –

Cover photographs:
special BLB classic R blue montage
kindly loaned by the Bicycle Store Paris.

LAURENT BELANDO

URBAN CYCLING

FROM THE BMX TO THE FIXIE

MITCHELL
BEAZLEY

PREFACE

Dear enthusiasts, bike lovers, and likely future readers of this fine book. The bike is familiar to us all: it makes us feel alive, takes us where we want to go, and is our daily companion. But which bike? There are so many, enough to meet the needs of every kind of user. It's an eclectic extended family, with some highly specialized members. We urban cyclists – accustomed as we are to streets, the pressures of traffic, and the beauty of the night – do sometimes dream of mythical mountain climbs, rides through wild country, and freedom. We are as impressed by cutting-edge technology as we are stunned by the extraordinary physical abilities of professional cyclists. But how does this all fit with our own use of the bike?

We belong to the city: we live, work, and move around in it. And our bike accompanies us through everyday life. That bike does its job – whether it's an electric bike that was bought new or a fixed-wheel bike, whether it has a freewheel or is a vintage steed. You don't hear people talk about our bikes much, but among ourselves we talk about them incessantly. For our bike matches us – you could even say it's an extension of our body: we and it are one, and it allows us to experience special sensations. Its clean lines and custom paint job express our creativity, and help us to be creative. It is beautiful, and we treasure it, proudly displaying it at home just for the pleasure of looking at it. It goes with our dress sense, and it influences us while at the same time identifying with us. So we're actually talking about a state of mind, a lifestyle – or simply a style, period.

The idea of creating a magazine as a vehicle for this culture and style, portraying its protagonists and their different roles, seemed obvious – even a need. *Steel Magazine*, now a mover and shaker in this urban cycling trend, has watched it develop, thanks to a varied readership and a growing number of visitors to its café. I am honoured to be writing a few words for this book by Laurent Belando who, like many of us, and from the moment he first turned a pedal, has never stopped seeking to find out more about the bike. It's an infinite subject – countless kilometres covered, encounters with other riders, and doubtless interminable post-ride discussions. So here is a worthy tribute to this modern phenomenon, which demands our attention and deserves to be showcased in a book.

Marc Sich
Publisher and editor
Steel Magazine

CONTENTS

P. 123

P. 167

TECH
CHOOSING YOUR BIKE –
ADVICE BEFORE YOU BUY

CYCLING DISCIPLINES AND TRIBES

p. 125
INTRODUCTION

p. 126
**MESSENGERS AND
ALLEY-CAT RACES**

p. 136
SPOKE CARDS

p. 138
CITY CRITERIUMS

p. 142
BIKE POLO

p. 148
FREESTYLE

p. 152
TRACK CYCLING

p. 156
MINI DROME

p. 158
CYCLO-CROSS

p. 162
GROUP RIDES AND EVENTS

p. 169
INTRODUCTION

p. 170
ARTISANS

p. 182
CHOOSING A FRAME

p. 186
**COMPONENTS TO
BE RETAINED**

p. 188
**CHOOSING REPLACEMENT
COMPONENTS**

p. 190
USEFUL INFO

p. 191
ACKNOWLEDGEMENTS

THE URBAN BIKE: FROM THE BEGINNING TO THE PRESENT DAY

FROM FREEWHEEL TO FIXED SPROCKET

> "THE BICYCLE, IN ITS MODERN FORM, CAME INTO BEING IN THE 1890s."

IT'S NOT SUCH AN OLD INVENTION

Because it's of fairly simple construction and mechanically undemanding, it might be tempting to think that the invention of the bicycle is as old as that of the wheel. However, it was only around 1818, some two centuries ago, that Baron Karl Drais invented the draisine, also known as the velocipede – universally recognized as the first two-wheeled vehicle powered solely by the rider's legs. Today, such contraptions are reserved for small children with little sense of balance. But it's amusing to imagine those early top-hatted riders, their backsides juddering on the long wooden beam that was the main structural element of the machine, with its two wheels resembling those of a cart…

It wasn't until some 40 years later that a Parisian locksmith named Pierre Michaux added pedals – at the suggestion of his son Ernest, who wondered what to do with his legs between strides. And it took another 20 years before the cranks, which until then had been attached to the front wheel, were moved to the frame and combined with a chain.

We can say that with the advent of the first contemporary frame, consisting of two adjacent triangles, in the 1890s, the modern bicycle – not unlike today's brakeless fixies, for it had no freewheel or derailleur yet – was born, just over a century ago. Even so, such was the bicycle craze at that time that the end of the 19th century saw a great number of discrete but major developments – the freewheel, removable tyres, gears, and so forth – leading to hundreds of patent applications for various design innovations.

THE CITY: BIRTHPLACE OF AN OLYMPIC SPORT

Today, it is probably hard to imagine just what a tremendous success velocipedes, bicycles, and penny-farthings were from the outset. At that time, Paris was home to so many historic firsts and premieres of international events that the city became the cradle of world cycling.

The whole world flocked to the city's Champ-de-Mars to gaze at the first velocipedes with pedals, on display at the second International Exposition of 1867. On 31 May 1868, the first official cycle race in history took place in the park of Saint-Cloud. Such was the level of enthusiasm that amateur races were organized all over the world. The first periodical devoted to cycling, *Le Vélocipède*, appeared on 1 March 1869, and many cities built velodromes. In 1893, Paris and its environs boasted more than 20 velodromes destined for sporting events and leisure cycling. Flush with this success, cycling was one of the nine sports at the 1896 Athens Olympics, the inaugural games of the modern era. There were five track events, won mostly by French riders, and one road event. All these races, naturally, were run on bikes with fixed sprockets.

"DURING THE SECOND WORLD WAR, THE BICYCLE BECAME A TOOL IN A DAY-TO-DAY EXISTENCE THAT WAS HARSH."

THE PENNY-FARTHING

Bikes with pedals attached to the front wheel, no gears, and champions who averaged less than 18km/h (11mph) … the first races in history were like contests run with children's scooters. Even the most basic modern example, stuck in first gear, could have thrashed these early machines.

Those pioneer record-holders were not content, and vied with each other in seeking ingenious ways to improve their steeds. It was James Moore, winner of the first race in history and of the first edition of the Paris–Rouen race, helped by a French artisan named Eugène Meyer, who had the idea of increasing the size of the front wheel to increase the distance travelled with each revolution of the pedals. It was probably the strangest and most fascinating invention in the history of the bicycle, and one we all remember: the penny-farthing.

11

A DEMISE FORETOLD

At the first international conference on the automobile held in 1900, Georges Forestier, possibly the first internationally recognized expert in the field, highlighted the crucial role cycling had played in the birth of the motor car. But he also announced his belief that the latter would dominate the former as time moved on. Nevertheless, throughout the first half of the 20th century, the bicycle became ever more widespread, reaching even the most remote rural regions. There are a number of reasons for this growth in popularity, but perhaps none more prominent than the fabulous image of cycling publicized by the highly popular Tour de France, launched in 1903 by Henri Desgrange and Géo Lefèvre.

"IN THE 20TH CENTURY, PARIS BECAME THE CRADLE OF WORLD CYCLING."

ALEXANDRE VOISINE

PROFESSION
Cycling designer

BIKE
Penny-farthing

MODEL NAME
RBR Superior 52"

FRAME	Steel
WHEELS	52in front/14in rear
HUB	Handmade, in titanium
RIM	Aluminium, made in UK
CRANKS	Three pedal positions, giving three effective crank lengths: 180mm, 155mm, 130mm
HANDLEBAR	Chromed steel
SADDLE	Ledder. Leather, with specially made rails
OTHER INFO	Replica of a Gormuly & Jeffery machine, built in San Francisco in 1880
AWARDS	European Champion 2014

Now, each member of the family had access to a bicycle, and people learned to ride from an ever earlier age. It was inconceivable that a little boy or girl wouldn't be taught to ride a bike. But the bicycle, which had become the household's main means of transport, was also associated with fun. It was used not only for travelling to work, but for going on holiday too. It allowed people to escape, to travel in the open air.

However, something was about to upset this peaceful stability. With the Second World War and the occupation of much of Europe, France, for so long the spiritual home of cycling as a pastime, found itself short of petrol and subject to harsh rationing. Cars were requisitioned for the war effort, and the bicycle became a tool in a day-to-day existence that was harsh. Consequently, it came to be associated with effort, constraints, and toil.

Moreover, after the war, the motor car became aggressively dominant. The newly liberated population wanted to turn a dark page in its history, and consequently deserted bicycles and public transport. People flocked to buy these new vehicles, symbols of a free Europe. In 1959, thanks to an industrial policy that strongly favoured the car, promoting massive investment in the road network and car production, bicycles were stowed away in cellars and attics. The idea of "a car for everyone", reinforced by the likes of Henry Ford, became the creed of the post-war years and was emblematic of the consumer society.

A symbol of prosperity and individual freedom, the car left less and less road space for the bicycle, which now was reserved for the poor and people on the fringes of society. Amateur races, tainted by gambling, also lost appeal for the public. And the bicycle industry, once so flourishing, collapsed.

MESSENGERS: THE STORY OF A RENAISSANCE

Although messengers themselves do not seem to know quite where, or why, the fixed sprocket returned to the limelight, there are a number of urban myths. The most widespread, though it comes in several versions, has it that the fixed sprocket was reintroduced in New York by a handful of bike couriers in the 1980s. Fed up with their bike components getting stolen or wearing out, they turned to track machines, which have no derailleurs or brakes – and therefore no cables.

The most credible version sets this development not in New York but in San Francisco. In 1970, that city, like everywhere else in the world, was choked with traffic. Pollution from cars was becoming a real public health hazard. The automobile, the previous century's dream, had become that century's trap. The city authorities, in order to promote walking and cycling, decided to install a vast network of cycle tracks. Some districts of the inner centre were even closed to cars. Too much noise, too much pollution, too much danger. It was a real awakening.

At that time, the job of bike messenger was something completely new. Jamaican couriers, who were very numerous in San Francisco, could not afford to equip themselves with expensive bikes, so they got the idea of using old track machines. Because they lacked technical refinements, these were much more afford-

"THESE DAYS, A FIXIE CAN COST SEVERAL HUNDRED, OR EVEN THOUSANDS."

able – and had the added advantage of being faster and more reliable than a normal bike. (Somewhat ironically, today a fixie can cost hundreds, even thousands.) New York, too, was the scene of this new trend. Both cities saw the use of the fixed-sprocket bike grow and flourish. In the process, it attracted the keen interest of the Early Adopters who, although they were not messengers (like the hipsters in Brooklyn) nevertheless saw it as a way of combining vintage style with environmental awareness. In France, this raising of awareness happened after a period of crisis and upheaval in 1968, and was triggered by the oil price shock. French people, who were seeking to get back to a healthy way of living, began to re-evaluate the place of the bicycle in the urban environment. However, nothing changed significantly until the appearance of the first self-service hire bikes – first put in place on a large scale in the city of La Rochelle – followed by the arrival of the foreign fixie phenomenon in the early years of the 21st century.

A NEW VISION FOR THE CITY

Today, the city bike is everywhere, with the fixie leading the charge – swarming through city streets, gracing the windows of luxury shops, and featuring on the pages of glossy fashion magazines. After finding its space on the internet – thanks especially to the videos posted by the famous Mash SF community, which was among the first to film a fixie in the same way as skateboarding – it now finds itself, like a film star, on the big screen. With Hollywood having sensed the public's growing interest in the phenomenon, it was no surprise to see Superman straddle a fixie to embark on a chase through the streets of Metropolis, or a New York bike messenger as the main character of the film *Premium Rush*.

The profession of bike messenger continued to grow relentlessly in big cities, as more and more people, both men and women, abandoned their climate-controlled offices for this unusual occupation – witness Jack Case, the trader played by Kevin Bacon in the mystical 1986 movie *Quicksilver*. However, beyond the undeniable fashion trend that has sprung up around the fixie and bicycles in general, a real philosophy of life and taking control of the urban space has been born, based on environmentally friendly principles, of which the bike is a cornerstone.

This philosophy consists of moving around free of public transport timetables, traffic congestion, and the need to find a parking place. A philosophy that empowers you to stop, or on the other hand lengthen your journey, as the mood takes you. A philosophy bound up with the wellbeing of a body accustomed to exercise and, above all, a general sense of satisfaction. A philosophy whose watchword is freedom!

"PEOPLE BEGAN TO RE-EVALUATE THE BICYCLE IN THE URBAN ENVIRONMENT."

15

"THE PROFESSION OF BIKE MESSENGER CONTINUED TO GROW RELENTLESSLY IN THE BIG CITIES."

CHARLIE CONORD

PROFESSION
Professional track cyclist

BIKE
Track

MAKE AND MODEL
Look 496

AWARDS

- 3rd, individual sprint, French Championships 2013
- 3rd, individual sprint, French Championships 2012
- Winner, individual sprint, World Cup, Beijing, 2012
- 3rd, keirin, French Championships 2011
- French espoirs champion, kilometre, 2009
- French junior champion, keirin, 2008
- World junior champion, team sprint, 2008 (with Thierry Jollet and Quentin Lafargue)
- World junior champion, keirin, 2008
- Silver medal, individual sprint, juniors 2008
- French champion, team sprint, 2007 (with Thierry Jollet and Kenny Cyprien)
- French junior champion, sprint, 2007

CHARLES

FRAME	Colnago World Cup
WHEELS	Mavic Ksyrium Disc
TYRES	Challenge Paris–Roubaix, for the cobbles of Paris!
CHAINSET	SRAM Red, the rest of the groupset is SRAM Force
HANDLEBAR	Carbon monocoque
SEATPOST	Deda, zero setback
SADDLE	fi'zi:k Antares

MIKA

PROFESSION
**Bike messenger
with Fahrwerk**

BIKE
Fixed wheel

FRAME	Aluminium
HANDLEBAR	Deda Pista
SADDLE	fi'zi:k Wing-Flex Vitesse Sport

BIKE TYPES

While a bike's main function is as a means of transport, today's cities have become the playground for a great variety of bikes, with sometimes very different characteristics, uses, and styles.

This resurgence of interest, which began on the west coast of the United States, originated by a handful of bike messengers and by groups such as the famous Mash SF, was largely driven by the resurgence and refinement of the fixie bike, with its stylish, stripped-down style. A true contemporary phenomenon. The creation of cycle paths and the provision of self-service rental bikes in large cities also contributed. This was a necessary development, closely connected to the desire to improve city residents' quality of life.

Although many have yet to take the bold step of embracing the fixed wheel – not least because it obliges the rider to learn how to pedal all over again – it is nevertheless the case that it has played a part in restoring the image of city bikes, single-speed machines, bikes with baskets, and other vintage machines that for too long had been gathering dust in deserted bike shops or in cellars and attics. It has even allowed a whole generation to discover, or rediscover, the joys of the road bike, through a different prism from the popular one of the Tour de France. For, if most urban cyclists choose to buy a road bike in addition to their city bike, it is because the former allows them to ride further and faster than with a fixed-wheel machine.

This book does not aim to be exhaustive, but it does contain the main groups of bikes that feature in the urban landscape. For, aside from the characteristics mentioned above, different bikes, though they may sometimes be seen as fashion accessories, are above all a reflection of their owners' personalities. So it is pointless to try to set out a catalogue: to each individual their own bike. Each forges a very personal bond with it and shares, as a member of a community inspired by the same passion, the pleasure of having specced their "steed", and the feeling of forming a team with it.

HANDLEBAR

You can find any type of bar on a fixie. Some prefer a track handlebar for its drop and its elegance. Others opt for a riser handlebar, which allows them to weave through traffic more easily. Yet others seek out the aggressiveness and versatility of a bullhorn or pursuit bar. Finally, there are those who go for a vintage touch with a moustache handlebar. With a fixie, the choice is yours – but a handlebar says a great deal about the owner.

THE FIXIE

Hugely popular with bike messengers since the 1990s, the fixed-wheel bike, also known as the "fixie", is a track bike for city use. Unlike the machines in your average bike shop, it has a rear sprocket that is fixed to the wheel, i.e. without a freewheel. Lacking gears and – if the laws of the country allow – often even brakes (in which case it's known as "brakeless"[1]), its rider is at one with the machine. Speed is controlled via the pedals alone.

KING OF THE CITY

This kind of riding is comparable to walking or running – it's instinctive and free. In city riding, contrary to what many believe, it can even give a greater feeling of safety than when riding a bike fitted with a freewheel.

LEARNING TO RIDE A BIKE AGAIN

Climbing onto a fixie can feel crazy and disconcerting. Nevertheless, the fixed-wheel bike has won a wide following for, once the technique of the skid[2] has been mastered, a rider generally quite soon comes to appreciate the freedom and control this kind of bike offers.

A FASHION ACCESSORY

Fundamentally, the passion for this new kind of cycling is closely linked to the almost "fetishistic" nature of the bicycle in itself. Besides the feeling of freedom, the fixie's devotees profess a particular affection for their bike, spending all the time and money necessary to make sure it resembles no other. The aesthetic of the bike is the very essence of the cult devoted to it. You build yourself a bike unlike any other, unique and in your own image: fast, if you love furious sprints across the city, rough if you want the messenger look, elegant if you co-ordinate the saddle and the handlebar tape[3] for a smart city look, and so on.

DID YOU KNOW?

The fixie is the only type of bike that can be ridden backwards. This discipline, known simply as "backward circles"[4] is one of the events that make up alley-cat races.[5] There is even a world championship.

27

1. Brakeless *refers to a bicycle that has no regular braking mechanism either via levers or back-pedal brake. It is usually a bike for use on the track, where brakes have been historically prohibited. In France, on the road, the law obliges bike owners to fit their machine with two "effective" brakes.*

2. Skid *(see page 130).*

3. Handlebar tape *is a band of leather or plastic that is wrapped, like a tennis racket grip, around the handlebars to improve grip and comfort.*

4. Backward circles *(see page 135).*

5. Alley-cat *(see page 126).*

JULIEN

PROFESSION
Dental prosthesist

BIKE
Fixed wheel

BIKE'S NAME
Concept bike

MAKE AND MODEL
Peugeot DL121

FRAME	Peugeot
GEAR	46 x 15 (3.07) (83in)
OTHER INFO	Concept bike DL121, built by the Peugeot Design Lab. Just ten units produced in 2012. This is no. 008. All aluminium and carbon components have been soaked in a copper-plating bath. Team: PARISCHILLRACING

DAVID

PROFESSION
Software architect

BIKE
Fixed wheel

BIKE'S NAME
The Shetland
(as in pony)

FRAME	Cinelli Vigorelli Caleido
WHEELS	Mavic Ellipse
CHAINSET	SRAM Omnium
HANDLEBAR	Deda RHM 02
SADDLE	San Marco Concor Red Hook Crit 2013
OTHER INFO	Frame was bought when it came out in March 2014, directly from MashSF

CÉDRIC

PROFESSION
Engineer

BIKE
Lo-pro with
fixed wheel

FRAME	BLB La Piovra Aero
WHEELS	Miche Versus
HUBS	Continental GP Classic
CHAINSET	Campagnolo Record Pista
GEAR	48 x 15 (3.2) (86in)
HANDLEBAR	3T 2002 Evol
SADDLE	San Marco Regale UP
SEATPOST	Miche Supertype

GREG
DE GUOJI

PROFESSION
Aeronautical mechanic

BIKE
Track (fixed sprocket)

BIKE'S NAME
Marie

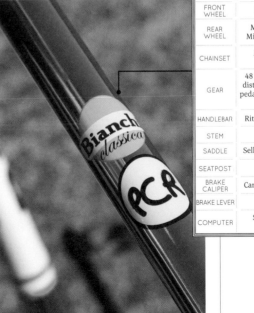

FRAME	Bianchi Pista Steal
FRONT WHEEL	Mavic Cosmos
REAR WHEEL	Mach 1 – 430 on Miche Primato hub
CHAINSET	Miche Primato Advanced
GEAR	48 x 15 (3.2 – actual distance travelled per pedal revolution, 6.7m) (86in)
HANDLEBAR	Ritchey Logic II WCS
STEM	Cinelli Pista
SADDLE	Selle Italia – Gel Flow
SEATPOST	Cinelli Vai
BRAKE CALIPER	Campagnolo Centaur
BRAKE LEVER	SRAM 500
COMPUTER	Sigma BC 16.12 STS CAD

FRAME	Moby cycles track
FORK	Carbon
FRONT WHEEL	Aerospoke
REAR WHEEL	B43 Velocity
CHAINSET	BLB track, aluminium
GEAR	46 x 17 (2.71) (73in)
HANDLEBAR	BLB drop
SADDLE	Nukeproof Trail

CARLOS

PROFESSION
Dentist

BIKE
Fixed wheel

FRAME	Cinelli Mash Bolt (Columbus Airplane tubing)
FRONT WHEEL	H Plus Son Archetype rim on Victoire hub
REAR WHEEL	Carbon (HED track sticker) on Novatec hub
CHAINSET	Sugino 75 with Sugino Zen NJS 47t chainring
PEDALS	Look S-Track
GEAR	47 x 15 (3.13) (85in)
HANDLEBAR	fi'zi:k Cyrano carbon
STEM	Thomson X2 10°
SADDLE	San Marco Zoncolan
SEATPOST	Cinelli Ram
OTHER INFO	Team: Ride Du Mercredi (Paris)

CLÉMENT

PROFESSION
Artistic director

BIKE
Lo-pro, pursuit

BIKE'S NAME
Medusa

FRAME	Handmade, brazed, sized for 700 front/ 650 rear wheels, with wishbone seatstays
FORK	Colnago 650 CX Aero
FRONT WHEEL	Campagnolo Shamal 650C, 18-spoke
REAR WHEEL	Mavic Cosmic
CHAINSET	Stronglight 107
GEAR	50 x 15 (3.33) (90in)
HANDLEBAR	3T bullhorn, cut off
STEM	3T
HANDLEBAR TAPE	Brooks
SADDLE	Brooks swift
SEATPOST	Shimano 600 Aero

YANN
AKA TOTARA
AKA DÉGLINGO
DU CIBOULOT

PROFESSION
Marketing manager/
graphic artist/
web designer

BIKE
Fixed wheel

FRAME	BLB Classic
RIMS	Mavic Open Pro
HUBS	Victoire Cycles, engraved with the word SURPLACE
CHAINSET	Campagnolo Record Pista
HANDLEBAR	Nitto B123AA Track Black Aluminium NJS
SADDLE	San Marco Vintage Rolls
SEATPOST	Miche Supertype Black
STEM	Nitto Jaguar
OTHER INFO	Team: SURPLACE

HANDLEBAR

Track, road, straight, moustache, riser, bullhorn, pursuit … as with a fixie, all are permissible. The only condition is that they should be fitted with two brake levers.

THE SINGLE SPEED

The fixie's little brother, the single speed, boasts all the same qualities: a stripped-down, minimalist frame with a very stylish city look, and, of course, a single gear, chosen according to one's daily rides and physical abilities. The only difference – and it's not insignificant – is that a single speed is fitted with a freewheel, with pedalling independent of the rear wheel. Power is transmitted from the chainset to the wheel, but never vice versa.

A REASSURING RIDE IN TOWN

Many consider a single-speed bike safer in town because braking happens in the traditional manner – via the brakes. This is a real advantage on descents, where the rider does not need to pedal. However, it is essential, as with any other bike fitted with a freewheel, to keep hands on brake levers in case of the need to stop – whereas, with a fixed wheel, unless the rider's feet are off the pedals, they are constantly monitoring speed and braking. A single-speed bike is often the choice of cyclists reluctant to make the psychological leap to a fixie.

FIXIE CULTURE

Since a single-speed rider displays all the characteristics, both in kit and in clothing, of a fixie rider, it is sometimes difficult to tell one from the other. Some single-speed riders, defying basic safety rules, even go so far as to leave out the rear brake. Others, more prudently, install a back-pedal brake instead.

39

DID YOU KNOW?

Many single-speed and fixie bikes on the market feature a so-called "flip-flop" rear wheel. This features a hub[1], which can be fitted with a sprocket at either end so that, if it is desired to change sprocket, all that's needed is to turn the wheel round. Originally conceived to accommodate two different gears[2] on the same fixie bike without having to remove a sprocket, this arrangement is widely used today to combine a fixed wheel and a freewheel on the same bike.

1. Hub: *central part of a wheel, where the spokes converge. This is where the sprocket or cassette (a cluster of several sprockets on a bike with gears) is fitted.*

2. Gear: *the ratio between the number of teeth on the chainring and on the sprocket. The smaller the gear, the more it is suitable for going uphill – and vice versa.*

RODOLPHE

PROFESSION
Visual artist/performer

BIKE
Single speed

BIKE'S NAME
My Fucking
White Horse

FRAME	Motoconfort, *circa* 1960–70
RIMS	Velocity B43 700C
HUBS	BLB Chrome
CHAINSET	Sturmey-Archer
GEAR	42 x 17 (2.47) (67in)
HANDLEBAR	Original – cut short/narrow
SADDLE	Original – leather cover

ROLAND

PROFESSION
Restaurant manager

BIKE
Single speed

42 ⟩

RIMS	Mavic
STEM	BLB

MARIE
AND ÉRIC

PROFESSIONS
**Project manager
and graphic artist**

BIKE
Single speed

MAKE AND MODEL
6KU Frisco 2

FRAME	High-tensile steel, TIG-welded throughout
RIMS	45mm Deep V alloy
HUBS	Quando flip-flop, 32-hole
GEAR	44 x 16 (2.75) (74in)
SADDLE	Selle Royal

OLGA

PROFESSION
Communications and
media manager

BIKE
Vintage city

‹ 45

FRAME	Unisex city bike
WHEELS	Track
CHAINSET	Single speed
GEAR	48 x 16 (3) (81in)
HANDLEBAR	Vintage moustache
SADDLE	Brooks B17 Standard Classic

HANDLEBAR

Road bikes are usually fitted with drop handlebars. This offers several positions for the hands, according to the rider's level of effort: several high positions for climbing or endurance riding, and lower positions for attacking (in a race, for example) and maintaining an aerodynamic position.

The more positions a handlebar offers, the lower the risk of numbness or pain in the hands. Road bikes used for time trials are often fitted with tri-bars – extensions that allow the elbows to rest on the handlebar, thus improving aerodynamics.

THE ROAD BIKE

To the uninitiated, the first image this term conjures up will doubtless be that made famous by the Tour de France. Sometimes, indeed, bystanders shout mock encouragement at people passing on road bikes, which will bring a smile to the rider's lips, especially if they happen to be riding a fixie...

A SPORTS MACHINE THROUGH AND THROUGH

The road bike, often referred to as a "racing bike", is the sports bike par excellence. Weighing as little as 7kg,[1] and boasting high-end equipment – clipless pedals, electronic gear shifting, carbon fibre frame, and so on – the road bike is designed to cover long distances at speed with the minimum of effort. Its wide range of gears (often more than 20) enables riders to climb mountains at considerable speed and without too much difficulty.

IN TOWN

A road bike can easily handle the steep hills that some cities have to offer. However, given the risks of vandalism and theft, using such a machine (whose price can also be extremely steep) in the urban environment seems risky. Nevertheless, such bikes are often seen in town. And recently, many fixie riders have taken to buying a road machine to escape from the city.

A SPECIAL SARTORIAL STYLE

Roadies[2] and their bikes have long been known for garish colours and tasteless graphics – as well as shaved legs, wraparound shades, and so on. Happily, things are changing, and now some brands offer products that combine refinement and high-end technical specifications.

DID YOU KNOW?

Although dedicated road riders shave their legs, this is neither in order to show their leg muscles to the best advantage, nor even to reduce wind resistance. They do this because it makes the massage of the thigh and calf muscles after a hard stage painless, and makes it easier to treat wounds suffered in the event of a crash.

47

1. The UCI (*Union Cycliste Internationale – world cycling's governing body) places a minimum weight limit of 6.8kg for competitors' bikes.*

2. The term 'roadie' *is used to denote cyclists whose sport is road cycling, as opposed to "trackies", who ride on the track.*

MAMZELLE'MO

PROFESSION
Costume designer

BIKE
Road

BIKE'S NAME
Titanium Donkey

MAKE AND MODEL
Frame
Merlin Cyrene with
engraved head tube

FRAME	Titanium (hence the bike's name)
WHEELS	Mavic Aksium Elite
CHAINSET	Shimano Ultegra, 11-speed
HANDLEBAR	Deda
SEATPOST	Deda
OTHER INFO	Adjustable stem

EMMANUEL

PROFESSION
Shop manager

BIKE
Road (set up
for endurance rides)

MAKE AND MODEL
LOOK 565
(repainted in Chevrolet
metallic black)

FRAME	LOOK carbon frame and fork
HAND-BUILT WHEELS	Campagnolo Omega rims
FRONT HUB	DT Swiss
REAR HUB	Campagnolo Chorus (from 10-speed groupset)
CHAINSET	Campagnolo Chorus (with Campagnolo Chorus bottom bracket)
STEM	Thomson 0°
HANDLEBAR	DEDA Zero 100 compact
SADDLE	fi'zi:k Arione
SEATPOST	Thomson

MATTHIAS

BIKE
Light touring

BIKE'S NAME
Gilberthe

MAKE AND MODEL
Gilles Berthoud Etna

FRAME	Gilles-Berthoud Etna custom (after its former owner)
WHEELS	Hand-built: VIA hubs, DT Swiss spokes, H Plus Son Archetype rims. Continental Grand Prix 4 Season tyres
CHAINSET	SRAM Rival
HANDLEBAR	Nitto B135 Grand Randonneur, 45cm
SADDLE	Brooks Cambium C15

JULIEN

PROFESSION
Graphic designer

BIKE
Road

MAKE AND MODEL
Festka One
Carbon, custom
hand-built in
Prague, Czech Republic

FORK	Columbus Grammy
WHEELS	Zipp
CHAINSET	SRAM Red
HANDLEBAR	3T
SADDLE	Specialized Romin Carbon Pro

HANDLEBAR

This type of bike is often fitted with so-called "moustache" or "straight" handlebars. These enable the rider to keep a relatively straight back and, consequently, to have a better view of the surrounding traffic. This is an ideal position in town. It also reduces the risk of sweat stains appearing on the rider's back, and puts less strain on the lower spine. There are various designs, but the top marks for elegance go to the retro, delicately curved "moustache" handlebar that, once fitted with leather grips, looks stunning.

THE CITY BIKE

55

This is the bike for everyday use – its style elegant and understated. It is proof that not all cyclists are high-performing athletes with muscular calves, and that it's not compulsory to choose one's bike according to one's body weight. The city bike, which is practical and doesn't get its rider dirty, is above all built for comfort. It features an ample, comfortable saddle, a small, delicate-sounding bell, mudguards, a chainguard, lights to see and be seen, and a frame often, somewhat outdatedly, referred to as being from a "lady's bike", because it can be straddled without raising the leg too high and splitting trousers or revealing a petticoat.

THE BIKE-SHOP OWNER'S FRIEND

The city bike is the machine that gets used every day to go from A to B, without worrying about getting your hands dirty. Therefore, it's also the bike of choice for those who don't necessarily want to learn how to change an inner tube or oil a chain. Its wheels are robust and its tyres usually puncture-resistant.

DID YOU KNOW?

The city bike underlines the difference between the utilitarian machine and the sports machine. Whereas the latter is aimed at pushing the rider's physical limits, speed, and heightened sensations, the former places emphasis on comfort and relaxed mobility. A sports bike is for climbing mountains and breaking records; a utilitarian bike is for avoiding them.

MAYLIS

PROFESSION
Financial advice tutor

BIKE
City, single speed

BIKE'S NAME
Gustave

MAKE AND MODEL
**Lygie Sprint
Saint-Étienne**

| FRAME | Cesare Rizzato & C., steel |

YANNIS

PROFESSION
Freelance art director

BIKE
City

BIKE'S NAME
Red is dead

MAKE AND MODEL
Anita Spranghina
Donna

FRAME	Lugged steel
CHAINSET	Shimano Nexus, with 5-speed hub gear
SADDLE	Brooks B17 black

VIDYA

PROFESSION
Freelance
graphic designer

BIKE
City

MAKE AND MODEL
Peugeot
Record du monde
(early 1980s)

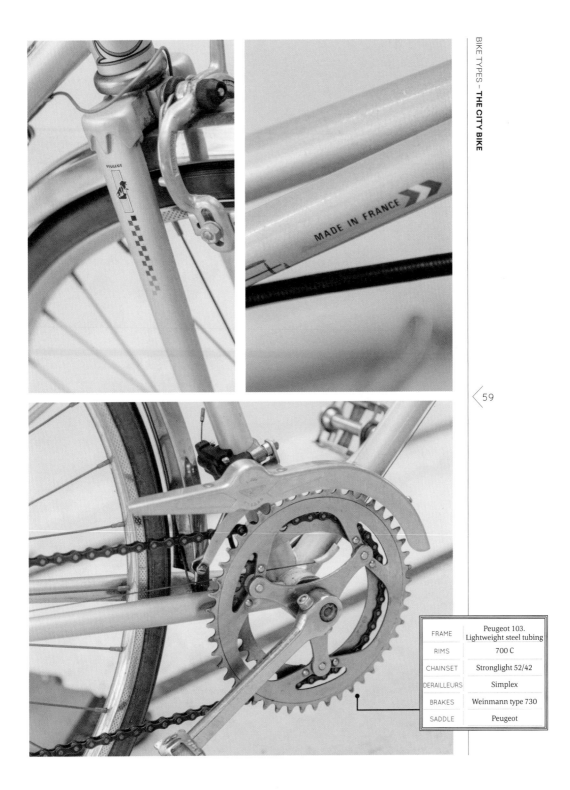

‹ 59

FRAME	Peugeot 103. Lightweight steel tubing
RIMS	700 C
CHAINSET	Stronglight 52/42
DERAILLEURS	Simplex
BRAKES	Weinmann type 730
SADDLE	Peugeot

AGNÈS

PROFESSION
Graphic artist

BIKE
City

MAKE AND MODEL
**Peugeot UE18
(late 1970s)**

FRAME	Peugeot UE18
OTHER INFO	Home-made luggage rack

LAURE

PROFESSION
**Consultant at Creative
Content Strategies**

BIKE
City

FRAME	G. GINET, steel
SADDLE	Brooks B15 Swallow, chrome
HANDLEBAR	Covered in Brooks leather handlebar tape

∿ HANDLEBAR

Vintage bikes are mostly fitted with a classic road handle-bar, whose geometry varies slightly from one country to another. Back in the day, there were Italian, Belgian, and French bars, and even Franco-Italian and Franco-Belgian ones...

THE VINTAGE BIKE

More than anything else, the vintage bike bears lively witness to the passion many of us have for the bicycle. It is part of us. We love the machines that are emblematic of our childhood, and adore the Tour de France and its great protagonists: Eddy Merckx, Bernard Hinault, Jacques Anquetil, Raymond Poulidor, and so on. The vintage bike is also the legendary bike of days gone by: the bombastic penny-farthing; the Hirondelle and its famous *rétro-directe* gear system; Bianchi bikes, with their inimitable blue-green paint; Mercier bikes; Peugeot bikes; and so on. Passionate owners refurbish such bikes with love.

Finally, it is the machine for owners who have retained a taste for the authentic. Such people find nothing more elegant than an old steel bike with down-tube gear levers, and feel nothing can equal the style of chrome forks, Christophe toeclips with leather straps, and light alloy Campagnolo brake levers, drilled to save weight.

IN TOWN

This type of bike is very popular in towns because it's an excellent choice for someone seeking a sophisticated, elegant, fast, and lightweight machine that can be bought for a very reasonable price. Some shops – such as La Bicyclette in Paris' 12th district – specialize in these machines, and offer spare parts and vintage bikes that have been completely refurbished.

For the past few years, however, with increasing demand, it has become ever harder to find old classic bikes in large cities, and some enthusiasts think nothing of travelling hundreds of kilo-metres to dig out rare gems in jumble sales or garage sales.

STYLE

As far as style goes, you can go completely retro and wear polka-dot clothes, braces, a beret, and a moustache for big events such as L'Eroica, a vintage cycling event in Tuscany (with offshoots in the UK, USA, and Japan) that attracts thousands of vintage enthusiasts from all over the world.

PRASSAY

PROFESSION
**Director of MODE PAP
– brand development**

BIKE
Fixed wheel

MAKE AND MODEL
**GANOLO –
Cycle Laurent**

FRAME	Ganolo
WHEELS	Mavic
HUBS	Maillard
CHAINSET	Miche
GEAR	47 x 15 (3.13) (86in)
HANDLEBAR	Philippe
SADDLE	Selle Italia Turbo Comp. vintage
SEATPOST	Campagnolo Competition vintage

JOHN

PROFESSION
IT engineer

BIKE
Vintage road

BIKE'S NAME
JJ Reicrem

MAKE
Mercier

FRAME	Reynolds 531 throughout
WHEELS	Mavic module 2
CHAINSET	Stronglight
HANDLEBAR	Belleri
SADDLE	Selle Italia Superleggera

FLORENT

PROFESSION
Artistic director at a publisher and co-founder of Ridekulture

BIKE
Vintage road

BIKE'S NAME
P.I.M.P.

MAKE AND MODEL
Peugeot PS10 Gold 1978
Reynolds 531

‹ 67

FRAME	Reynolds 531 tubing, size 58. Stronglight competition headset
WHEELS	Mavic
CHAINSET	Nervar, 52/42
HANDLEBAR	Philippe
STEM	3T
BRAKE CALIPERS	Mafac 2000 Gold

LAURA

PROFESSION
Independent editor,
author of the book
A Gloriosa Bicicleta
(Texto).

BIKE
Road

BIKE'S NAME
Brigitte Peugeot

MAKE AND MODE:
Peugeot
Record du Monde
PBN10 (early 1980s)

FRAME	Peugeot 103, lightweight steel tubing
RIMS	700C
BRAKE LEVERS	Dia-Compe
MUDGUARDS	Velo Orange Martelé 35mm
SADDLE	San Marco Corsaire 313

WIDEN
VON DEN
ZORGEN

PROFESSION
Cash handler,
Banque de France

BIKE
Road, steel frame

MAKE AND MODEL
Unknown

FRAME	Custom, built 1991. Vedett paintwork
RIMS	Omega Strada Hardox
HUBS	Campagnolo Record
CHAINSET	Campagnolo
GEAR	42/52 chainrings, road cassette
HANDLEBAR	3T Gimondi Competizione, recently embellished with Brooks handlebar tape
SADDLE	Idéale TB90 Spéciale Compétition, treated with the Daniel Rebour process
SEATPOST	Campagnolo Chorus Aero

VINCENT

PROFESSION
Lawyer

BIKE
Road

MAKE AND MODEL
Raymond Clerc,
2nd generation –
mid-1980s

FRAME	Dural, one-piece tapered fork without reinforcement. Internal cable routing
WHEELS	Campagnolo Super Record with large-flange hubs
CHAINSET	Campagnolo Super Record
HANDLEBAR	Cinelli
SADDLE	San Marco Rolls

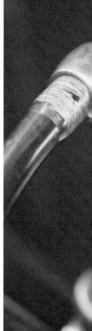

HANDLEBAR

Conversion bikes are fixies and, as such, may be fitted with all kinds of handlebars. However – and this small detail unfailingly sets them apart – conversion bikes, like track machines, often boast a quill stem. Although especially elegant, this type of stem has been replaced on most modern machines by the threadless (A-head) design which, though markedly less good-looking, is lighter.

THE CONVERSION BIKE

This is a vintage bike that has been "converted" into a fixie or single-speed machine. When the first fixies appeared on the streets, it was sometimes hard to find components for this new cycling style. Manufacturers had not yet had time to respond to this new market, and track bikes weren't easy to find everywhere. As the number of riders of this type of bike grew rapidly, so the conversion of old road bikes into fixies became common.

Today, it has become much easier to buy fixies off the peg. Nevertheless, there are many riders who go down the conversion route, chiefly for reasons of cost. Some manufacturers have seen their business boom by offering all kinds of individual components. One example is Brick Lane Bikes (BLB), which originally was a small bike shop in East London but which, over just a few years, has become a flourishing business and a leader in this field. Almost any frame will pass muster, as long as enough time is invested. It is even possible, pushing the principle to the limit, to build a fixie bike entirely out of salvaged parts.

IN TOWN

A conversion is an ideal day-to-day bike for city use. These machines have "lived", and so are less vulnerable to dents and rust. They are also, in general, less attractive to thieves. But beware – sentimental attachment to a bike is often far stronger if you've seen it take shape, born of the work of your own hands...

DID YOU KNOW?

The resurgence of vintage bikes among hipsters was part of their urban, trendy image, and the craze for converting these old machines to a fixed wheel was what gave rise to the term "fixie".

DOMINIC

PROFESSION
Cycle messenger

BIKE
Conversion

BIKE'S NAME
Berta

FRAME	France Cycles, circa 1980. Found in the street
FRONT WHEEL	Found in the street
REAR WHEEL	Bought second-hand for €20
CHAINSET	Original
GEAR	48 x 16 (3) (81 i.)
HANDLEBAR	Salvaged from Vélorution (a network of co-operative bike workshops)
SADDLE	Found in the street

GWEN

PROFESSION
Sales assistant in a
wines and spirits shop

BIKE
Fixed wheel

BIKE'S NAME
Tortellini

FRAME	Regazzoni Varese 1978. Columbus SLX tubing
FRONT WHEEL	Rigida Nova
REAR WHEEL	Halo Aerotrack
HANDLEBAR	Win Japan – cut off
GEAR	44 x 15 (2.93) (79in)
SADDLE	fi'zi:k Nisene

DELPHINE

PROFESSION
Artist

BIKE
**Road – with
fixed sprocket**

MAKE AND MODEL
Flandria, 1970s

HANDLEBAR	SOMA Walker Racer Bar
BRAKE LEVER	Dia-Compe
PEDALS	Lyotard-Berthet
TOESTRAPS	Christophe
STEM	Pivo
SADDLE	Excelsior, leather

BERTRAND

PROFESSION
Shop manager

BIKE
Conversion – fixie

BIKE'S NAME
Legacy

FRAME	Motobécane, 1980s
FORK	Aluminium/carbon
WHEELS	700C
RIMS	Carbon, deep profile – 88mm, fitted with 23mm tyres
HUBS	Novatec free/fixed
HANDLEBAR	Road
SADDLE	BLB Aero
OTHER INFO	Old 1980s road bike frame converted into a fixie

HÉLOÏSE

PROFESSION
Engineer

BIKE
Conversion – fixie

79

FRAME	Bernard Carré
WHEELS	Campagnolo Zonda. Rear hub replaced with a Miche Pista (fixed-wheel hub)
CHAINSET	Peugeot
HANDLEBAR	Road – cut off and upturned. Home-made leather grips
SADDLE	Vintage, leather

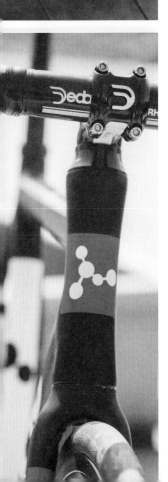

THE TRACK BIKE

This is the bicycle in its purest form: a frame, two wheels, a handlebar, pedals, and a saddle. Nothing else. Simplicity in the service of performance. When you press on the pedals, you get something animal back – as if the beast was hungry for power and speed. This sensation, characteristic of the fixed wheel, is, furthermore, reinforced by the complete absence of brakes. The whole bike seems to have been designed never to stop. Brakes are even regarded as dangerous on a cycling track; if a rider in a bunch applied them, it could cause a sudden pile-up of all the other riders. However, behind this apparent simplicity, the track bike – like the road machine – is packed with technology. Flying round the banked curves of the velodrome at more than 50km/h (31mph), these bikes need to be extremely stiff to withstand the rider's power and steer accurately. Each component of the bike has been refined to transfer as much of that power as possible and to optimize aerodynamics. It is common to use disc wheels or "monocoque" aerodynamic wheels with a small number of flattened spokes rather than conventional spoked wheels, in order to increase the flywheel effect and therefore the bike's performance.

IN TOWN
One might think that a track bike is totally unsuitable for city use. Nevertheless, many fixed-wheel enthusiasts who value high performance ride around town on this type of machine. Indeed, this trend is what gave rise to urban criteriums (see page 138).

81

DID YOU KNOW?

Despite the lack of gears and brakes, track machines are very often heavier than their road counterparts. This is because the stresses generated by acceleration in sprinting demand that the carbon fibre from which the frame is built be reinforced, to retain its stiffness. So, for example, whereas a road bike can easily come in below the 6.8kg minimum allowed, the bike used by François Pervis, multiple world champion on the track, tipped the scales at 7.2kg.

SIMON

PROFESSION
Digital project manager

BIKE
Fixed wheel, brakeless

BIKE'S NAME
René Charles

FRAME	ARGON 18 ELECTRON aluminium
FORK	ARGON 18 E-99 carbon
WHEELS	Mavic Ellipse
CHAINSET	SRAM Omnium
CHAINRING	Factory 5
GEAR	47 x 14 (3.36) (91in)
HANDLEBAR	Deda RHM 01 compact road
SADDLE	BLB Aero CroMo
SEATPOST	Deda RSX 01
WEIGHT	7.7kg
OTHER INFO	Headset top cap: Da Bomb

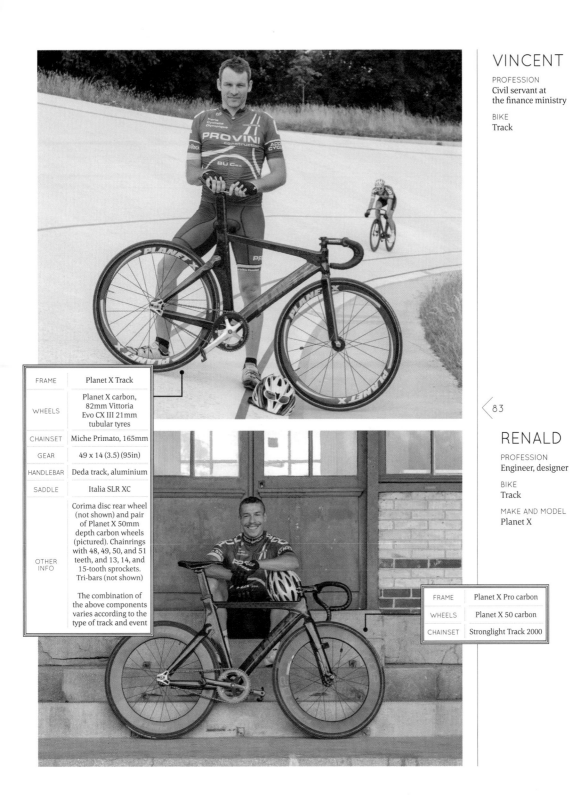

VINCENT

PROFESSION
Civil servant at
the finance ministry

BIKE
Track

RENALD

PROFESSION
Engineer, designer

BIKE
Track

MAKE AND MODEL
Planet X

FRAME	Planet X Track
WHEELS	Planet X carbon, 82mm Vittoria Evo CX III 21mm tubular tyres
CHAINSET	Miche Primato, 165mm
GEAR	49 x 14 (3.5) (95in)
HANDLEBAR	Deda track, aluminium
SADDLE	Italia SLR XC
OTHER INFO	Corima disc rear wheel (not shown) and pair of Planet X 50mm depth carbon wheels (pictured). Chainrings with 48, 49, 50, and 51 teeth, and 13, 14, and 15-tooth sprockets. Tri-bars (not shown) The combination of the above components varies according to the type of track and event

FRAME	Planet X Pro carbon
WHEELS	Planet X 50 carbon
CHAINSET	Stronglight Track 2000

THE COMMUTER BIKE

What we now refer to as a "commuter" bike has almost always existed – it just wasn't called that. Originally, the term was used in the United States to refer to people who lived on the outskirts of cities and travelled a certain distance regularly. Nowadays, the meaning has evolved and now denotes anyone who travels to work – and the number of people who do so by bike is increasing hugely in cities around the world. And although the term "commuter" could apply to any type of bicycle in this book, thanks to successful marketing it now refers specifically to compact and folding bikes.

The term also applies to a whole range of accessories and clothing specifically designed for day-to-day use of the bike – anything from waterproof jeans with reinforced seams complete with a loop for attaching a lock, to a waterproof, breathable jacket with reflective strips, or town shoes with concealed pedal cleats[1].

85

IN TOWN

The folding bike needs no parking facilities once you have arrived at your destination – it's easy to stow and unobtrusive. Once folded, not only can it be slipped under a desk or into a cupboard with ease, but it doesn't get in the way on public transport in the rush hour.

Many different types exist, for manufacturers have always sought to make bikes foldable and transportable, vying with each other in finding ingenious ways to reduce to the minimum the time it takes to fold a bike, and the space it occupies once folded. Modularity is a key principle for this type of bike, which must be able to accommodate a bag or a briefcase without flinching.

DID YOU KNOW?

The British brand Brompton – which makes the folding bike by which others are judged – organizes an annual world championship for riders of its machines. This competition is well known for its standing start in which competitors must wait for the word "go" before unfolding their bikes – echoing the start of the famous Le Mans 24-hour motor race.

1. **Pedal cleats** *are a system that enables the shoe to be rapidly attached to the pedal, on a principle similar to ski bindings. They give a more efficient pedalling action and, unlike toeclips and straps, are safer in the event of a crash, as they automatically release the foot.*

CÉDRIC

PROFESSION
Web editor

BIKE
Commuter

BIKE'S NAME
Patrick Pratique

MAKE AND MODEL
Brompton S2L

FRAME	Steel, in racing green (except for grey forks and rear triangle, and black stem)
REAR HUB	Two-speed: 13 and 16 teeth
CHAINSET	Shimano Dura Ace 7400, with Spécialités TA Alizé 54-tooth chainring
HANDLEBAR	Easton EC70 (carbon)
SADDLE	Selle Italia SLS Flow Kit Carbonio
SEATPOST	Brompton + 6 cm
SHOCK ABSORBER	Birdy vert (less comfortable but stiffer)
HEADSET	Tange alu
PEDALS	Shimano PD-A600
BRAKE LEVERS	Tektro RL720
OTHER INFO	Titanium mudguard stays, Garmin Edge 800 GPS, Crane brass bell, Brompton S-Bag, Schwalbe Kojak tyres, Minoura SBH-300 bottle cage bracket, Minoura AB100-5.5 bottle cage

HANDLEBAR

If the basket or rack is at the front, it's best to go for a riser, straight, or moustache handlebar.

THE PORTER BIKE

This is a nostalgic and evocative breed of bike, conjuring up a poetic image of easy living. When ridden in the open air, this bike makes you feel as if you've sprouted wings, and any journey takes on the character of a relaxed jaunt along a scenic riverbank, with a picnic and bottle of rosé wine in the basket.

Such bikes are equipped to carry shopping or other items – either with a simple rack over the front or rear wheel, or with a more sophisticated system of baskets or bags.

Originally, these machines were the preserve of certain jobs, and were used for deliveries – for example, by the celebrated Parisian newspaper delivery boys of the early 20th century, and the no less celebrated postmen. It is so handy to be able to carry small loads on a bike that today many machines have such equipment fitted as standard. Equally, it is a very simple matter to install a rack on most bikes.

DID YOU KNOW?

For a number of years, designers of all kinds have vied with each other in coming up with new and original bike transport systems, such as wine bottle holders, document holders, six-pack holders and, of course, the Tablet holder...

ROMAIN

PROFESSION
Restaurant manager,
event promoter

BIKE
City

BIKE'S NAME
Jacky

FRAME	Peugeot 103 Grand Tourisme – PX40M
HANDLEBAR	ATAX
SADDLE	GES
OTHER INFO	Former postman's bike. When it was found it still had the original leather bags. These bikes were produced between 1979 and 1983

LUCILLE

PROFESSION
Student in
international law

BIKE
City – women's model

BIKE'S NAME
Roberto

FRAME	Peugeot PH 45
WHEELS	Original
GEAR	46x16 (2.88) (78in)
HANDLEBAR	Original
SADDLE	Peugeot – original

ÉLISE

PROFESSION
Admin manager

BIKE
City – fitted with racks

BIKE'S NAME
Lily porteur

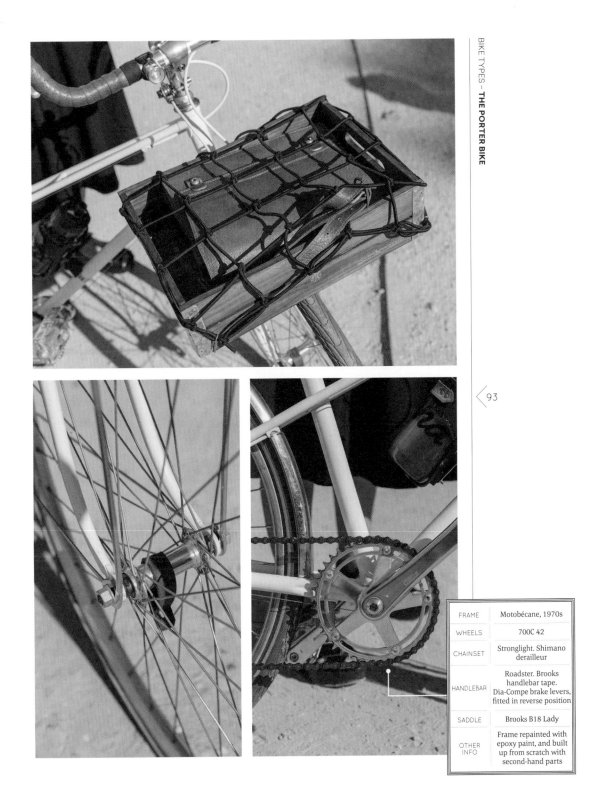

FRAME	Motobécane, 1970s
WHEELS	700C 42
CHAINSET	Stronglight. Shimano derailleur
HANDLEBAR	Roadster. Brooks handlebar tape. Dia-Compe brake levers, fitted in reverse position
SADDLE	Brooks B18 Lady
OTHER INFO	Frame repainted with epoxy paint, and built up from scratch with second-hand parts

JULIEN

PROFESSION
Businessman

BIKE
City –
electrically assisted

MAKE AND MODEL
ThirtyOne
Debut E-matic

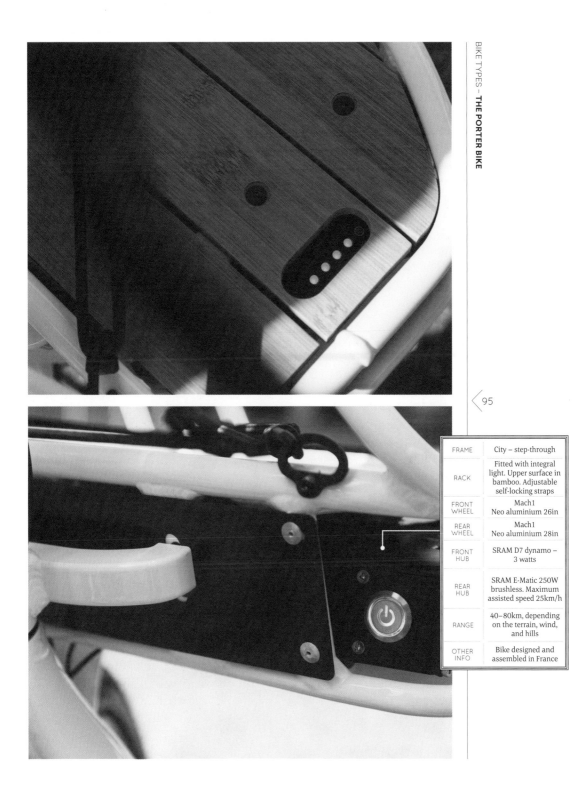

FRAME	City – step-through
RACK	Fitted with integral light. Upper surface in bamboo. Adjustable self-locking straps
FRONT WHEEL	Mach1 Neo aluminium 26in
REAR WHEEL	Mach1 Neo aluminium 28in
FRONT HUB	SRAM D7 dynamo – 3 watts
REAR HUB	SRAM E-Matic 250W brushless. Maximum assisted speed 25km/h
RANGE	40–80km, depending on the terrain, wind, and hills
OTHER INFO	Bike designed and assembled in France

MATHIEU
AND ANNE-
CHARLOTTE

PROFESSIONS
Artistic director
at DDB NYC

BIKE
City

MAKE AND MODEL
Abici Granturismo
Sport

FRAME	Steel, hand-built in Italy
REAR HUB	Sturmey-Archer, 3-speed
SADDLE	Brooks Swift
OTHER INFO	Vélo Orange front rack, retro-fitted

LÉA

PROFESSION
Shop assistant at
Cycles Get Lost

BIKE
Fixed wheel

BIKE'S NAME
Ginette

MAKE AND MODEL
oRa Cycles, "raw" model

FRAME	Steel, brazed
WHEELS	Mavic Module E rims, Normandy front hub, BLB track rear hub. Cross 3 spoke pattern
CHAINSET	Sturmey-Archer, 144 BCD, Factory 5 chainring, slate
CHAIN	Izumi gold
GEAR	47 x 17 (2.76) (75in)
HANDLEBAR	BLB Bullhorn, silver
SADDLE	Brooks Cambium C17S rust

HANDLEBAR

Traditionally, this type of bike is fitted with a straight handlebar, which offers better manoeuvrability and balance.

THE CARGO BIKE

As its name suggests, the cargo bike is a large machine that can carry heavy loads at the front or the rear. There are two main categories: the two-wheeled type, configured like a traditional bike, and the three-wheeled type, which is a tricycle.

The two-wheeled design is by far the more common today because, though bulky and naturally heavier than a traditional bike, it retains all its characteristics. Its centre of gravity is very close to the ground, which makes it highly manoeuvrable. It is fast and easy to handle; some models can carry loads of more than 200kg while still being as comfortable as a traditional bike. That's easily enough to carry, for example, the rider and two or three children in perfect safety. Or the rider and a washing machine...

Although very popular in many countries until the 1960s, this type of bicycle has almost completely disappeared, replaced by cars. It is still widespread in northern European countries such as the Netherlands and Denmark, where it is an integral part of the culture. For example, there were still some 40,000 cargo bikes in the greater Copenhagen area in 2011.

Despite its decline, the cargo bike is seeing something of a revival, and this growing popularity is no longer confined to couriers, who traditionally used it in large numbers to transport goods. For this type of bike has also gradually become the vehicle of choice for families seeking an alternative to the motor car to take their children to school or carry their shopping. Moreover, most brands offer equipment specifically for carrying children, such as seats, hoods, and so on.

HIGH SPECIFICATIONS

The Bullitt and Omnium brands deserve a mention. They have taken the small world of cargo bikes by storm, offering models whose light weight and level of equipment are worthy of a road bike.

DID YOU KNOW?

There is a highly active community that organizes annual cargo-bike meetings and races worldwide. The Cycle Messenger World Championships even features an event especially for cargo bikes.

JULIEN

PROFESSION
Cycle mechanic
at Cycles Get Lost

BIKE
Cargo

MAKE AND MODEL
Bullitt

FRAME	Bullitt custom paint
WHEELS	Rigida BigBull rims, Alfine and Shimano Deore hubs
CHAINSET	SRAM Apex CX
HANDLEBAR	BLB Big G Bar
SADDLE	Brooks team pro (pictured). Brooks C17 in normal use

ALEXIA

BIKE
Cargo

MAKE AND MODEL
Bullitt Bluebird

FRAME	Bullitt, fitted with a seat and cover for carrying children

HANDLEBAR

Because of its extremely squat, low-slung design, the BMX bike is fitted with a special, rather high handlebar, which echoes the shape of those used in motocross and is reinforced with a horizontal bar.

THE BMX

The BMX ("bicycle motocross") bike appeared at the end of the 1960s, a time when extreme sports were growing. As its name suggests, it is directly inspired by motocross, which was highly popular at the time. It is said that teenagers, unable to afford motocross, tried to imitate that sport right down to the smallest details of the clothing used.

BMX bikes have a freewheel and no gears. Very similar to a single-speed machine, they are, however, much more agile and manoeuvrable, thanks to their small size and 20-in wheels.

Some BMX bikes are fitted with a freecoaster system[1], which allows them to be ridden "fakie"[2], that is, backwards, without the cranks revolving.

Originally developed for jumping over obstacles on dirt track courses, the BMX bike soon proved useful for performing tricks and getting over urban obstacles, even holding its own against skateboards and rollerblades in skateparks.

105

IN TOWN

BMX bikes are totally at ease in an urban environment, thanks to their great manoeuvrability. However, they are used mainly for leisure, because the bike's small size, saddle on which it is difficult to sit, and very low gears make it impossible to cover any distance in comfort.

DID YOU KNOW?

The BMX bike burst into popular culture in 1982, when Steven Spielberg gave it a central role in the famous chase scene in his film *E. T. The Extra-Terrestrial*. Its young heroes, who cross the city leaping all manner of obstacles, finally taking flight over a line of police thanks to the little extraterrestrial's help, are none other than the stars of the BMX scene at the time, including Bob Haro, Mike Buff, R.L. Osborn, and others.

1. Freecoaster: *an ingenious system in the rear hub that disengages it so that the cranks do not turn when the wheel is rotating in reverse.*

2. Fakie: *a term borrowed from boardsports, denoting riding in reverse on a bike equipped with a freewheel. In the case of a fixed-wheel machine, the term "backward" is preferred.*

MATHIS

PROFESSION
Sales assistant

BIKE
BMX Street

FRAME	Cult Chase Hawk 21in
HANDLEBAR	Shadow Vultus 9.5in
FORK	Shadow Captive
CHAINSET	Eightyfour P2
HUBS	Proper Magnalite
RIMS	Alienation Deviant
SADDLE	Combo Diamondback

MELVYN

PROFESSION
Professional BMX rider

BIKE
BMX

MAKE AND MODEL
KHE Adam Kun Pro

FRAME	KHE 19
WHEELS	KHE, with Geisha freecoaster, which allows the rear wheel to rotate in reverse unhindered by the pedals
CHAINSET	Autum Bikes
HANDLEBAR	KHE FlatBar
SADDLE	Odyssey

HANDLEBAR

On a beach cruiser, the handlebar is often a wider, more upswept variant of the roadster handlebar. The handlebar is crucial to the special look of a beach cruiser. To achieve a more "lowrider" style, you can opt for an extremely upswept version of this handlebar. Guaranteed to be a head-turner.

THE BEACH CRUISER/ LOWRIDER

This is the ideal machine for chilling. It's a heavy bike with a very comfortable seated position and large tyres known as "balloon tyres". It was invented in the United States in the 1930s to imitate the look of motorcycles, and it was the most common type of bike in the country until the 1960s. Thanks largely to their balloon tyres and laid-back character, cruiser bikes are still widely used around beaches, especially in San Diego, where they may be fitted with a device that allows the rider to transport a surfboard. This new role has produced the nickname "beach cruiser", and is one of the main reasons why this type of bike has seen a resurgence since the 1990s. There is also a variant, known as a lowrider, which aims to look like a chopper motorcycle[1], with a very long front fork and a seated position almost at ground level.

This type of bike's often considerable weight (more than 20kg), single-speed transmission, and wide tyres mean it's limited to flat terrain and is therefore unsuitable for wider city use – which explains why there are so few around. Nevertheless, a beach cruiser will certainly get you noticed.

DID YOU KNOW?

The beach cruiser supposedly inspired the first mountain bikes.

1. Chopper: *a type of American motorcycle with an extremely long fork.*

CODIN

PROFESSION
Student

BIKE
Beach cruiser

MAKE AND MODEL
Sparker Special 3i

FRAME	6061-T6 Aluminium
REAR HUB	Shimano Nexus 3-speed

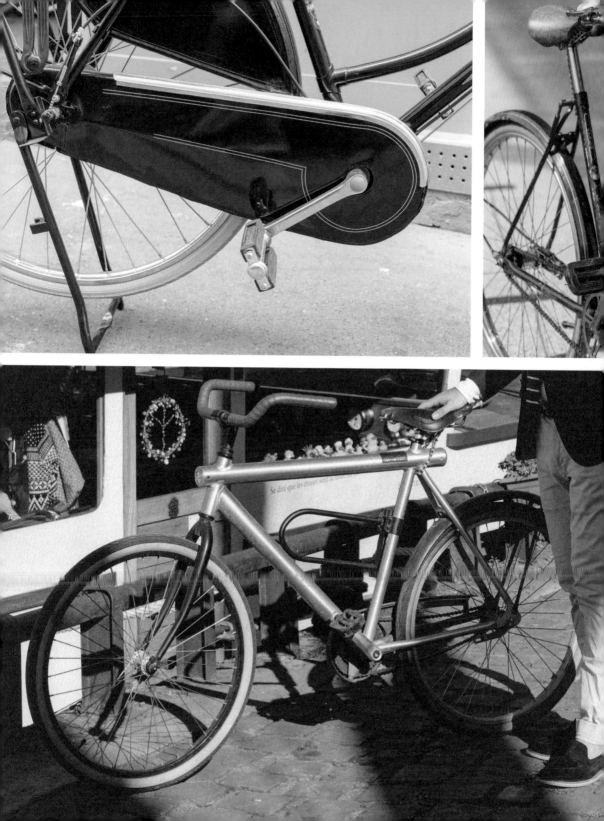

THE DUTCH BIKE

You can't really talk about urban cycling without mentioning the Dutch bicycle. This elegant, proud machine, black from head to foot, is typical of the city of Amsterdam, and the Netherlands as a whole. Originally from that country, as its name suggests, this unique bicycle has won many devotees all over the world. In the collective unconscious, it is the very model of the city bike and urban mobility.

ROBUST AND COMFORTABLE

The Dutch bike is a large machine with an upright pedalling style. The handlebar rises upwards, keeping the rider's back straight and increasing comfort at low speeds.

Designed to spend as little time as possible in the bike repair shop, the Dutch bike is geared to withstand the elements and the ravages of city life. Mechanical parts are oversized to make them more robust. The lack of gears, plus brakes that are either the drum or back-pedal type, mean the bike requires virtually zero maintenance.

Like the city bike, to which it is closely related, the Dutch bike also spares its rider discomfort, being lavishly equipped with a broad saddle, mudguards, skirt guard, enclosed chain guard, and so on. One peculiar detail that it often features is a lock integrated with the frame that, when closed, makes the bike unrideable by blocking the rear wheel.

A HEAVYWEIGHT

However, all this equipment and its robust construction inevitably have a bearing on the bike's weight. Although this is not a major problem in a flat country such as the Netherlands, the Dutch bike would not be an easy ride in a hilly town.

DID YOU KNOW?

Thanks to a less steep seat tube angle, on a Dutch bike it is much easier to put a foot to the ground without dismounting than on other types of bicycle.

THIBAUT

PROFESSION
Communications
consultant

BIKE
Dutch

MAKE AND MODEL
Vanmoof

114 >

HANDLEBAR	Substantially upswept, for a proper Dutch position
SADDLE	Brooks Team Pro Classic

OLIVIA

PROFESSION
Architecture student

BIKE
Dutch

BIKE'S NAME
Diego

DRIVETRAIN	Single speed, with back-pedal brake
SADDLE	Iscaselle Tornado
BELL	Fuuvi Charly

SABRI

PROFESSION
Shopkeeper

BIKE
Dutch

MAKE AND MODEL
Gazelle Toer Populair

FRAME	Steel
WHEELS	28-inch (40-635)
CHAINSET	Steel
GEARING	3-speed hub gear
BRAKING	Rod-activated hub brakes
SADDLE	Brooks B66, leather
OTHER INFO	This brand has existed for more than 120 years

THE VÉLIB'®

Few nations have such a connection to the bike as the French, and few cities embrace that in the same way as Paris – and the Vélib'® is the symbolic proof of this relationship. A hassle-free, city-wide bike rental system, the Vélib'® has made cycling available to absolutely everybody in the urban environment. And if this fine example of urban mobility, which continues to find imitators world-wide as more and more cities adopt similar cycle-hire schemes, has been relegated to the end of this chapter, it is only because, unlike the other bikes described in this book, it is not a unique, personalizable object that one would be proud to flaunt. Nevertheless, the self-service hire bike is a real step forward in urban mobility. It favours usage over ownership. The main thing isn't to have an attractive Vélib'® bike, because they are all identical and grey, but to have collective access to bikes for moving around town. It's far removed from a consumerist approach: people no longer talk about "taking my bike" but simply refer to "taking a bike".

Owning your own bike is generally no bar to subscribing to Vélib'® or any similar scheme. Many of the urban cyclists featured in this book subscribe to a public bike scheme as well as riding their own machine.

Aesthetically, Paris's Vélib'® bike is unquestionably the work of designers with tortured minds. Heavy (22.5kg) and hard to manoeuvre, the riding experience is not too far removed from straddling one of Pierre Michaux's velocipedes dating from 1890. But that is the price to be paid in order to have access to bikes all over town, at an extremely reasonable cost, and at all times, without having to worry too much about where to park them or the risk of theft. So, all in all, it is a fine invention.

DID YOU KNOW?

The companies that run these bike hire schemes organize a number of events every year. Other initiatives include a competition that consists of hiring a Vélib'® at the bottom of the steep rue de Ménilmontant in Paris, and dropping it off at the top, in as little time as possible. The hire ticket must be produced as proof of the time taken.

GUILLAUME

PROFESSION
Supervisor at the
central registry

BIKE
Public rental

MAKE AND MODEL
Vélib'®

YOUR HANDLEBARS SAY A LOT ABOUT YOU...

FLAT BAR

You use your bike every day, but you're not necessarily after high performance. You like things to be simple and uncluttered but, while you're at it, prefer to have a decent pair of brakes too. You dress according to the latest trends and you never forget your Fahrer cycle clips (made from recycled plastic) so that your chinos don't catch on the chain.

TRACK

Born for the track, your bike is nothing less than a missile. You don't do things by halves – you charge into the traffic, head down, with your messenger bag on your back and your Krypo lock in your back pocket. In town, no one gets past you.

ROAD

You're ready to tackle long distances. For you, performance is everything, and you'd never go out without your padded shorts and skintight Rapha Lycra jersey. Your shoes are fitted with cleats, obviously.

BULLHORN

With this close cousin of the track bar, you subscribe to the appropriate dress code and aim for speed in city riding. However, you are judicious and adaptable, preferring to keep an eye on the traffic around you. Nevertheless, your choice of handlebar betrays your competitive temperament.

MOUSTACHE

You yearn for outings in the fresh air. Your style is amiable and relaxed. Canvas shoes and trousers above the ankle for him, pleated skirt and straw hat for her.

RISER

You like to be in control no matter what the situation, and to weave through the traffic. You think nothing of bunny-hopping onto a pavement. Your Bermuda shorts reveal your tattoos.

ROADSTER

With this British-style bar, you like to look down on all you survey. You have a stiff upper lip and show the traffic who's boss. In all circumstances, your style is impeccable, and you cannot allow yourself a single lapse of taste. Your brogues are a marvellous match for your Brooks leather handlebar tape.

BMX (OR FREESTYLE)

The city is your playground. Nothing in the world would induce you to swap your Vans shoes for a pair of pedal cleats. You have that skater look: baseball cap and T-shirt in summer, beanie and hoodie in winter.

CYCLING DISCIPLINES AND TRIBES

With the resurgence of bikes in cities, and as the number of devotees grows, the streets have witnessed the birth of new, purely urban disciplines over the past 20 years.

Driven by the ever-growing cycle messenger community and the renewed interest in fixed-wheel bikes, these have carved out a place for themselves in a cycling landscape that had long been dominated exclusively by the road-racing style of the Tour de France and Giro d'Italia.

After having taken over – often in an anarchic way – streets, car parks, sports grounds, or concert halls, these new disciplines have become structured, organized, and in some cases even professionalized, in order to deal with their runaway success. Some are very new – such as alley-cat races, where the aim is to navigate across the city, mirroring as closely as possible the job of the cycle messenger. Others, such as urban criteriums, hardcourt bike polo, and the mini drome, have been inspired by old disciplines, which have been updated for modern tastes and adapted to today's urban environment. Even sporting disciplines, such as track cycling, which were formerly extremely popular but have since become the preserve of a minority, have seen the numbers taking part growing for the first time in many years.

The momentum shows no signs of slowing, and its effects are now being seen outside the centres of cities. Riders are increasingly moving beyond the fixed wheel and turning to cyclo-cross and road bikes, participating in events that often take them far from cities. From simple night rides to alley-cat races run across a whole region, these meetings, organized online through social media, are often an opportunity to share the pleasure of riding with other enthusiasts. They are a sociable way of improving one's riding and increasing one's knowledge – and they often end with a convivial drink.

MESSENGERS AND ALLEY-CAT RACES

What does a messenger do when not at work? They play at messengers! In a sense, that's the simplest way to sum up what an alley-cat race is. For these are urban navigation contests that mimic the messenger's job. Originally only messengers took part, but for some years now they have been open to non-messengers. However, they remain extremely dangerous for those who are not hardened to weaving through traffic.

STICKING TO THE MANIFEST

At the start, a "manifest"[1] is issued to competitors. This is like a road map, showing the various checkpoints the rider must stop at. It's rather like the itinerary of a bike messenger's typical day. The winner is the first competitor to have visited all the checkpoints and presented his/her manifest at the finish.

Riders are graded according to pure speed but also, above all, their knowledge of the city. At the start of an alley-cat race, there may be several minutes during which no rider mounts their bike. Each is poring over a city plan to identify, based on the manifest, which is the quickest route.

CHECKPOINTS ARE ALL ABOUT SURVIVAL

Checkpoints are comparable to delivery addresses, and come in several different forms. Simple checkpoints merely demand that the competitor take note of some information or get their manifest stamped. Others reveal important information that does not appear on the manifest, such as the address of a hidden checkpoint. Pick-up checkpoints are where competitors must collect a parcel to be delivered at a "drop-off" checkpoint. Then there are "rush" checkpoints, which close at a certain fixed time.

Some checkpoints – called task checkpoints – test competitors, who must complete certain actions before continuing the race. They may be asked to climb and descend stairs several times with an armful of parcels, ask a passer-by to take their picture, or down a shot of alcohol in one. These challenges are limited only by the fertile imagination of the race organizers, and the harshness of the marshals at the checkpoints themselves...

Alley-cat races are particularly dangerous, because they are run at a breakneck pace in city streets, where it is not uncommon to see competitors cross intersections at speed, slaloming through cars and motor scooters.

COMPETITIONS

Every year, the elite of international cycle messengers comes together at the Cycle Messenger World Championship (CMWC). This consists of several different events, including an alley-cat and a main race that, unlike the former, is held on a closed circuit whose course is revealed a few days before the event. Competitors are therefore able to know in advance the location of checkpoints and the itinerary to be followed. At the start, competitors are issued with two different manifests. They have a total of three hours in which to cover as much of these as possible. The fastest competitors may even find they are issued with a third manifest.

Paris, which will host the CMWC in 2016, has since 2014 held, as a taster, the Boss2Paname competition, a Parisian championship of eight alley-cat races held over the course of a year. There are three categories of rider: messengers (open to all, but competitors must be either messengers or former messengers), non-messengers, and women, whether messengers or not.

There is no need to ride a fixed-wheel bike to take part in an alley-cat race. That said, some fringe events at alley-cat races cannot be entered with a freewheel – for example, the skid, track stand, backward circles, and footdown, all of which are a reminder of the historic ties between the fixed wheel and the world of cycle messengers.

THE SKID

This technique – which consists of braking by locking the rear wheel, causing the bicycle to skid – is a basic skill for riding a fixie, especially if it is brakeless. It is also an event, in which the distance skidded by competitors is measured.

In order to skid, the rider must transfer their weight as much as possible onto the front wheel, to reduce the friction exerting force on the rear wheel, and therefore on the pedals. The rear wheel's adhesion to the ground is thus less, and it is possible to prevent the pedals from turning. At this point, the rear wheel locks and the bicycle brakes. The less adhesion, the easier the skid – and the less effective the braking action. In general, competitors prefer to have the foot they use to touch the ground forwards, but the reverse can be the case.

As with the long jump in athletics, competitors have a certain distance to build up momentum approaching the start line – beyond which, of course, pedalling is forbidden. The winner is the rider who skids furthest. Some skid specialists can cover more than 100m (330ft).

THE TRACK STAND

This consists of remaining stationary on the bike without putting a foot to the ground – rather like a tightrope walker. This feat – made easier by the fact that it is possible to pedal backwards with a fixie – appears to defy the law of gravity, and the skill is quite widespread. Cyclists who perform track stands in town tend to impress passers-by and motorists, who observe them with astonishment.

To perform a good track stand, it is important to learn some basic rules before you can find the right position for your centre of gravity, which will enable you to hold your balance. First, the cranks must always be horizontal – one foot forward, the other back.

Second, the front wheel needs to be held at a slight angle (between roughly 35 and 65 degrees) and – most importantly – turned towards the side of the leading foot. This is the ideal position. All you need to do now is press on the pedals so that the bike moves slightly backwards and forwards, in order to keep your balance. In general, leaning slightly "inwards" – towards the side of the leading foot – and preferably remaining seated can both help.

In a competition, all the riders start together, with both hands on the handlebars. Any competitor who puts a foot to the ground is immediately eliminated. To make things harder, the umpire progressively orders competitors to remove a hand, then the other, then a foot, then the other, and so on. The last rider still upright wins. Sometimes competitors are asked to remove items of clothing as well.

CLÉMENT LEROY

PROFESSION
"Trackstander"
and showman

BIKE
Fixie – track

BIKE'S NAME
Bleu-Blanc-Rouge

FRAME	Stevens Arena
WHEELS	Corima, 4-spoke
CHAINSET	Stronglight, 50t
HANDLEBAR	3T Sphinx
SADDLE	fi'zi:k
AWARDS	• World record holder, 50km backwards: 2 hours, 48 minutes, 8 seconds. Set in 2001 at the age of 13 • World champion, track stand, 2013 • World champion, best trick, 2013 • World champion, track stand, 2015

BACKWARD CIRCLES

This consists of riding your bike in reverse – something that's only possible on a fixie. In competition, riders sit on their machines in the normal way and ride in circles backwards. The rider who executes the most circles wins. This is one of the most difficult events, demanding mastery of balance and great agility.

FOOTDOWN

Footdown isn't a technique, but a real test of agility. All the competitors gather within a circle formed by the spectators. Their goal is never to touch the ground with a foot. Unlike in the track stand, they are not obliged to remain stationary, and are allowed to push other riders with their bike. They can also jump slightly to keep their balance or change direction. Things get more interesting when the umpire asks the crowd to close the circle tighter. The last rider upright wins.

SPOKE CARDS

Spoke cards are an integral part of bike messenger and fixie culture. It is not uncommon to see, around town, bikes with these small laminated cards wedged between spokes.

Sometimes highly artistic and creative, spoke cards perform several different functions. In alley-cat races, they are the equivalent of the race number used in conventional events. Handed out to riders when they sign on at a race, they identify a competitor and enable them to be issued with a number. However, spoke cards are less important than the manifest, and a competitor who loses their spoke card will not be disqualified as a result.

Unlike a race number, they are not retained only for the duration of the event, and can become collectors' items. A sort of trophy, they are a mark of belonging to bike messenger culture, and bear witness to the rider's merit, for it is generally assumed that a messenger whose wheel is stuffed with spoke cards is a very good rider.

TAROT OR POKER?

The very first spoke cards are said to have been ordinary playing cards; the rider's number was written on the card. This tradition continues, but playing cards have given way to cards printed with the colours of the relevant alley-cat race, and they are generally laminated to render them more durable. Since alley-cat races even today are often unofficial, these cards are always preferred to conventional race numbers, because they attract far less attention and are viewed by police merely as original and decorative.

CITY CRITERIUMS

With the increased use of track bikes in big cities, new forms of cycle sport took shape and, with them, a new kind of race: the fixed-wheel race – or, an updated, urbanized, and extreme version of the criteriums of days gone by.

1. *redhookcrit.com*

2. *rad-race.com*

NO BRAKES, NEVER STOP...

These races – which began in the United States with the Red Hook Crit[1] and then took off in Europe with the Rad Race[2] and European editions of the Red Hook Crit – are not ordinary criteriums. Like skateboarding and other urban sports that came before, these events are not modelled on any other competition. However, they share certain features. First and foremost, they are races for fixed-wheel bikes. Technically speaking, these are the same machines that are used in velodromes, but the parallel ends there, for these races are run in an urban setting, on uneven road surfaces. The first Red Hook Crits were held at night in the streets of the Red Hook neighbourhood of Brooklyn, where traffic was banished, without official authorization, by a handful of volunteers. Another feature – and an important one – that these races share is a spirit of openness and accessibility. They are open to all, both experienced racers and mere enthusiasts, as long as they have a fixed-wheel bike.

Snobbery and machismo have no place here. Indeed, the very first Red Hook Crit was won by a woman, Kacey Manderfield, who left all her male fellow competitors trailing in her wake.

The success of city criteriums is undeniable. In less than six years, major cultural centres – Milan, Barcelona, Berlin, London, and Puerto Rico – have also held such races.

HOW THE RACES WORK

Generally, each race has its own rules. However, the original Red Hook Crit in Brooklyn, and the three editions held in Milan, Barcelona, and London – as well as the French version, National Moutarde Crit[3], work on the same principles. The 200 competitors are grouped into four qualifying pools, each of which has 30 minutes to record the best lap time they can. The 100 fastest race in Final A, which is a traditional race over 30km (18½ miles). The 100 slowest race in Final B, over 20km (12½ miles).

In Germany, by contrast, the Rad Race operates an elimination system. Pool races to qualify for the final are held over four laps. After each lap, the last competitor is eliminated. In the final, held over seven laps, the last rider remaining in the race wins. The Rad Race is an especially spectacular event, being held indoors on a karting track.

< 141

3. *nationalmoutard ecrit.com*

BIKE POLO

Bike polo, which has been held on grass for as long as bicycles have existed, is thought to owe its current format to bike messengers. In the late 1990s a group of messengers in Seattle, USA, began to adapt the rules of bike polo to its new urban environment – in the same way as happened with street hockey. In breaks between deliveries, they would take over tennis courts, street hockey pitches, basketball courts, or parking lots. These gatherings rapidly gained popularity, and a new urban discipline was born: hardcourt bike polo. Although hardcourt bike polo is hardly ever played using fixed-wheel bikes today, its history is nevertheless closely tied to the fixed wheel, and the vast majority of top players started out using one.

1. Mallet: *in bike polo,
as in traditional polo, the
mallet's head is mounted at
right angles to the handle.
It is used to control or strike
the ball. The length
of the handle is generally
in proportion to the height
of the cyclist.*

RULES

Like traditional bike polo, hardcourt bike polo is played using a mallet[1]. However, unlike the former, in which teams number five players, the latter is three-a-side and played on an enclosed court measuring 40 x 20m (130 x 60ft), with a plastic street hockey ball. The winning team is the one that scores five goals first – or the one with the highest score after 10 minutes' play. There are two historical rules. The "foot down" rule prohibits a player from continuing to play if their foot has touched the ground. That player must then stop playing immediately and touch one of the two extremities of the median line with their mallet before they can resume

playing – a manoeuvre known as a "tap out". This rule renders hardcourt bike polo spectacular, because it forces players to perform some acrobatic feats. The second rule stipulates that, for a goal to count, the ball must have been struck with the end of the mallet's head, not the side, which is reserved for controlling or passing the ball. Other rules have been added over the years, regarding interference, the area in front of the goal, and so on, but the sport is still young, and constantly evolving. Both the rules and players' level of skill have developed rapidly. Today, there are more facilities than in the past, and tournaments, attracting ever more sponsors, are better organized.

Both in Europe and in the United States, there is a drive to draw up new rules to make the sport even more attractive. Many tournaments try to put forward new formulae for the game: longer matches with no limit on goals and allowing substitutions compulsory platform pedals to reduce contact, a ban on interference, and so on.

This section was written with the help of Paul Vergnaud (see opposite), world champion 2011, 2012, and 2014, and European champion 2012, 2013, and 2014.

PAUL VERGNAUD

PROFESSION
Bike shop manager

BIKE
Polo bike

MAKE AND MODEL
Riding in Circles
(Italy), custom

FRAME	Custom-built frame with S & S couplers, which allow the frame to be dismantled
WHEELS	48 spokes. 2mm DT Swiss spokes
CHAINSET AND BOTTOM BRACKET	White Industries
GEAR	32 x 18 (1.78) (48in)
HANDLEBAR	Easton OS – straight
SADDLE	Brooks C15 Cambium England
AWARDS	• World champion 2014, 2012, 2011 • European champion 2014, 2013, 2012 • French champion 2014, 2013, 2012, 2011 • 2nd, World Championships 2013 • 2nd, French Championships 2015
SPONSORS	Chunk Clothing Brooks Riding In Circle Perro Del Mallet Milk Hoser

ALEX
VALCKO

PROFESSION
Webmaster at
Bicycle Store

BIKE
Polo bike

BIKE'S NAME
Riding in Circles

FRAME	Riding in Circles – Italian custom brand
WHEELS	Velvet Bikes 48-hole rims on White Industries M16 disc brake front hub and BLB rear hub
CHAINSET	Rotor mountain bike crankset, Hope chainring, Chris King bottom bracket, in red
GEAR	1.65 (45in)
HANDLEBAR	Easton EA50
SADDLE	San Marco Zoncolan UP
SEATPOST	Thomson Masterpiece
MALLET	MILK (Mallet I'd Like to Kiss)
OTHER INFO	Team: "The Birds", with Morgan from Lyon and Dodi from Budapest
AWARDS	• 2nd, French Championships 2013 • European champion, bench minor • 2nd, French Championships 2014 • 3rd, European Championships 2014 • Paris champion 2014 & MVP • French champion 2015
SPONSORS	Riding in Circles, San Marco, MILK

FREESTYLE

Freestyle, in a similar way to freestyle skate-boarding and rollerblading, is a discipline that involves using the bike to perform tricks. There are various kinds of freestyle including, in an urban context, flatland and street.

FLATLAND

This is to cycling rather what figure skating is to ice-skating – but without the tights and sequins. The discipline consists of performing a sequence of artistic movements on a flat surface, often balancing on one wheel, and without ever putting a foot to the ground. Riders rest their feet on pegs fitted to either end of each hub in order to create these positions. The discipline requires a high degree of co-ordination and a keen sense of balance.

In flatland, the BMX bike is king, for its short wheelbase and small wheels are a great advantage in performing movements. However, some riders prefer to use a fixie – though this practice is tending to disappear, as the possibilities offered by a BMX machine are so much greater.

In competition, contestants are judged according to the complexity, variety, and elegance of their movements.

STREET

Unlike flatland, street does not confine itself to flat surfaces. Here, the goal is to make maximum use of street furniture – benches, walls, steps, handrails, and so on – to perform tricks exactly as a skateboarder would. The basic manoeuvre is the bunny hop, which consists of making the bike jump without the aid of a springboard. This discipline has many adherents, who use both a BMX bike and a fixie.

Street competitions are held in skate parks, where obstacles and ramps replace street furniture, and allow far more aerial manoeuvres to be performed than in a pure street environment.

TRACK CYCLING

Although much less "alternative" than the previous disciplines, track cycling is nevertheless one of the great classic urban cycling disciplines – and is by far the oldest. Today, with the resurgence of fixed-wheel machines on city streets, it is regaining momentum.

More and more urban cyclists are rubbing shoulders with track riders. And the discipline – which has seen so many velodromes disappear – now appears to be seeing a turnaround in its fortunes. France is leading the way in this regeneration, and has built a flagship group of four super-velodromes in recent years. London's Olympic velodrome is also open to the public, offering a top-quality facility at a very affordable price. Meanwhile, in Paris, the restoration of the famous La Cipale track, which used to host the finish of the Tour de France before it was transferred to the Champs-Élysées, has just been completed, despite a number of setbacks and the threat of demolition.

BIG GEARS

Track cycling comprises a number of events, all involving fixed-gear bikes. They are many and varied, but can broadly be grouped into two categories. The first comprises sprints (both individual and team), the kilometre, the women's 500 metres, and the highly popular keirin race (a Japanese import), which includes several events for fast, powerful riders. The other comprises endurance races, including individual and team pursuit, the points race, the American relay, and finally the scratch races – events run over distances between 4km (2½ miles) and 50km (31 miles), and which demand the greatest endurance from riders.

MINI DROME

A mini drome is a track exactly like a conventional velodrome: oval in shape, with a wooden surface and curves banked at 42 degrees. The only difference – and it is a significant one – is that, as its name suggests, it is no bigger than 14 x 7m (46 x 23ft). And we might as well say loud and clear – as did the Austrian energy drink company whose brainchild it was – that it's the smallest velodrome in the world. Launched in New Zealand by Red Bull®, the idea rapidly caught on in European cities, and today it is no longer exclusively the domain of the founding company. In fact, not all mini dromes are the same size. The angle of the banking may be different from that of the track built by the Velotrack company[1] for Red Bull®. The Véloscope[2] in Toulouse, for example, is twice as big.

Since it can be dismantled and is relatively compact, the Red Bull® mini drome can be transported anywhere in the world – for example, to the pit of the La Cigale concert hall in Paris, or to the Brooklyn Masonic Temple.

A SPECTACULAR SHOW

As in a traditional velodrome, races are open only to fixed-wheel machines. Laps are ridden at breakneck speed, and riders crash out of the track frequently and spectacularly. In order to stay in contact and not lose power, competitors have to literally hurl themselves into the inside of the track's bends. The best riders favour a fixed-gear freestyle (FGFS) bike fitted with a very wide freestyle handlebar and 26in semi-balloon tyres, which are more manoeuvrable.

The gears used are between 2.4 and 2.7 (65–73in), depending on the rider's fitness level and on the track. In a competition, qualifying rounds are held. These take the form of time trials in which riders – riding alone on the track – must record one of the 32 best times to make it to the finals. Qualified competitors then take part in one-to-one pursuit races over ten laps. The best riders can cover that distance in 33 seconds[3]!

In Paris, the Red Bull® mini drome has welcomed all manner of famous racers, such as Thibaud Lhenry, world champion at the Red Hook Crit 2014; Mathias Danois, triple world BMX flatland champion in 2008, 2009, and 2011; and Damien Michalec, a specialist in the discipline, as well as track cycling champions such as Charlie Conord, Michaël D'Almeida, and Grégory Baugé, whose titles are too numerous to list here.

1. Velotrack *is a German company that specializes in building cycling tracks certified by the UCI (Union Cycliste Internationale).*

2. Véloscope *is a 1,000-m² (10,763-ft²) complex on the outskirts of the French city of Toulouse, entirely devoted to bikes, where exhibitions and events are held.*

3. This time *was recorded in a semi-final at the Red Bull® mini drome in Utrecht, Netherlands.*

CYCLO-CROSS

Cyclo-cross is a discipline that could be compared to mountain biking, but it is much older, dating from the 1950s. It consists of a bike race held off-road, often in woodland or through fields. The course is rendered more arduous by obstacles, which regularly force riders to carry their bikes slung over their shoulders.

Unlike a mountain bike, a cyclo-cross machine is similar to a road bike, and therefore has no suspension. However, it differs from a road bike in having a reinforced frame, wider tyres with a knobbly tread, and cantilever or disc brakes, to reduce the risk of mud building up between the wheels and the frame. It may also be fitted with a fixed gear or single freewheel, in which case riders inevitably prefer to run rather than ride up uphill sections.

As this discipline has regained popularity, some riders have competed against mountain bikes in events where this is allowed. Cyclo-cross bikes have the advantage on smoother terrain, while mountain bikes get the upper hand in the rougher uneven sections.

In cities, cyclo-cross is very popular at the moment, even though it isn't really considered an urban sport. Many fixed-wheel riders in search of new experiences have invested in a cyclo-cross bike to take part in amateur races organized near large cities. Such events are held in a relaxed, party-like atmosphere.

GROUP RIDES AND EVENTS

RIDING TOGETHER

Since riding a bike is even more fun in company, virtually all cities host at least one informal cycling event, often organized online and via social media. There is no need to belong to a club or association, as these rides are often open to all. The meeting place, time, and course map are generally publicized in advance online. These gatherings made their appearance at the same time as the fixie craze was taking off on city streets.

1. *londonnocturne.com/index*

2. *parischillracing.com* and *facebook.com/groups/ parischillracing*

3. *facebook.com/groups/ ridedumercredi*

4. *street-pistard.tumblr.com*

5. The Tweed Run *is a gathering of cyclists who wear traditional English dress, such as tweed jackets and trousers: tweedrun.com*

6. L'Eroica *runs sportive rides for lovers of vintage bike races: eroica.cc*

7. *anjou-velo-vintage.com*

NOCTURNES

This is the most widespread type of city ride. Nocturnes are weekly or monthly group rides over about 30km (18½ miles), traditionally held on weekday nights because city traffic is lighter then. This also allows riders to meet up after work. Many groups exist to organize this type of riding meet-up, so if you're interested, then you should fairly easily be able to find a local group. In London, you can try London Nocturne[1], or in Paris the main rides of this type are organized by Paris Chill Racing[2] and le Ride du Mercredi[3].

By contrast, some other rides are the preserve of riders with big gears and strong legs. Again, Paris has a strong showing of this kind of group, as evident in events such as the Street Pistard[4], held on a Tuesday, with itineraries of 40–60km (25–37 miles) outside Paris.

VINTAGE EVENTS

These are a variation on themed rides. Inspired by the Tweed Run[5] in London and L'Eroica[6] in Italy and various locations around the world, these day-long events are an opportunity to put on period clothing, dust down berets and pleated skirts, and mount one's old bicycle, polished up for the occasion. Every year the biggest of these rides, such as the Anjou Vélo Vintage[7] in France, brings together several thousand people from all over the world.

WEEKEND RIDES

City cyclists regularly meet at weekends for longer rides – also motivated by the same desire to get together with others for the fun of riding as a group. Often, such events are also an opportunity to picnic out in the countryside or to ride a different machine from the day-to-day one. Many rides are organized by groups and can often focus as much on the social aspect of the event as the cycling – invariably, these routes will end at a local brewery or café for riders to rest, relax, and socialize.

There are, of course, more sport-oriented setups as well, which tend to cover a distance of at least 100km (62 miles) on any given ride – compared to the more genteel distances of around 60km (37 miles) covered by the more social groups.

POLITICAL RIDES

Long predating fixie rides, these political gatherings have been very popular since the 1970s.

On the last Friday of each month the strongly anti-car Critical Mass movement, founded in 1992 in San Francisco, offers an opportunity to raise awareness of ecological, environmental, and citizenship issues. Other more original movements, such as the World Naked Bike Ride, run events in which participants ride unclothed to protest against dependence on fossil fuels and to celebrate the power of the human body.

1. *facebook.com/groups/ granfondoparisiens*

2. *rocknrollin.org*

3. *surplace.fr*

4. *velorution.org*

TECH

CHOOSING YOUR BIKE – ADVICE BEFORE YOU BUY

So, are you ready to take the plunge?

By now, you may have a better idea of the steed you need. But that's just the start of the adventure, because it's no simple matter to find your dream bike. In making your choice, you need to take into account three factors: your budget, your mechanical skills, and how much time you can devote to it. The first option that comes naturally to mind is to buy an off-the-peg machine in a shop. This will usually enable you, for a medium-to-high outlay, to acquire a bike quickly and to ride it straight out of the box. Nevertheless, bear in mind that a bike – even one manufactured on the other side of the world – still has an irreducible cost that will vary according to the quality of materials used and of its manufacture. Therefore, do not hurriedly choose a low-end machine whose weight and flimsy equipment may quickly lead you to get rid of it. Buying second-hand is an attractive alternative if you are on a very tight budget. However, as with a cheap new bike, it's advisable to have your prospective purchase checked over by a professional before deciding to buy.

If you'd rather forge a stronger bond with your bike, you might want to have it custom-made by an artisan. This option is more expensive and takes longer – you might be too impatient to get out and ride to stand the wait – but it nevertheless offers a great many advantages. It goes without saying that riding a bike perfectly tailored to your body shape will be more enjoyable, whatever the circumstances. Moreover – contrary to received wisdom – whether it is made of steel, titanium, or bamboo, such a bike will often be every bit as light and stiff as its industrially manufactured counterparts in carbon or aluminium. And unlike them, it will retain these characteristics over time.

Finally, an option favoured by many urban cyclists is the conversion of a vintage road bike into a single-speed or fixed-wheel machine. This route is more the preserve of bargain-hunters with mechanical skills, who are prepared to spend long hours in close contact with their future steed. But it allows you to build yourself a high-performance, reliable, and robust bike for a very affordable price. Be wary, though, of the potential pitfalls when choosing your frame and the various components that will make up your bike. The final part of this section will help you find your way.

169

ROBIN

PROFESSION
Co-founder of the
[In'Bô] brand

MAKE
[In'Bô]

INFO

This group of friends and enthusiasts founded the [In'Bô] brand, which specializes in working in wood and in outdoor sports equipment. A young company, it has demonstrated that with the use of modern techniques, wood, and especially bamboo, can be a high-performance material. Thibaut Lhenry won the 2014 Red Hook Crit on a bamboo bike, competing against professional teams who were riding aluminium machines. As well as making bikes out of bamboo from Anduze in southern France, the workshop also produces skateboards and sunglasses made out of wood from the nearby Vosges mountains.

JULIAN

PROFESSION
Nurse and
old bike restorer

MAKE
Santa's Workshop

INFO

It was during a stay in Melbourne, Australia, that Julian discovered, by chance, the art of restoring old bikes. While there, he proved to have a fine touch with the restorations he carried out for the Mottainai Cycles workshop. On his return to his native Biarritz, Julian amassed in his garage a hoard of cycling gems that he hunted down in between surfing and doing his job as a nurse. In the end, he set up his own bike restoration business: Santa's Workshop.

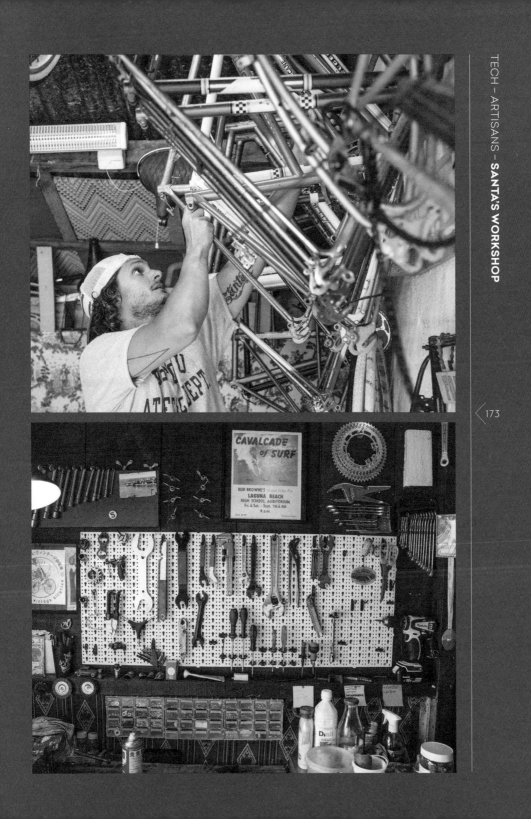

JULIEN

PROFESSION
Co-founder of the
Victoire Cycles brand

MAKE
Victoire Cycles

INFO

Julien founded Victoire
Cycles in early 2011,
aiming to offer high-
performance, high-end,
custom-made steel bikes
built in France. Having
learned the ropes by
making fixed-wheel
bikes, Victoire Cycles
quickly branched out
into other types. Today,
it produces high-end
road bikes, mountain
bikes, and cyclo-cross
and touring machines.

174

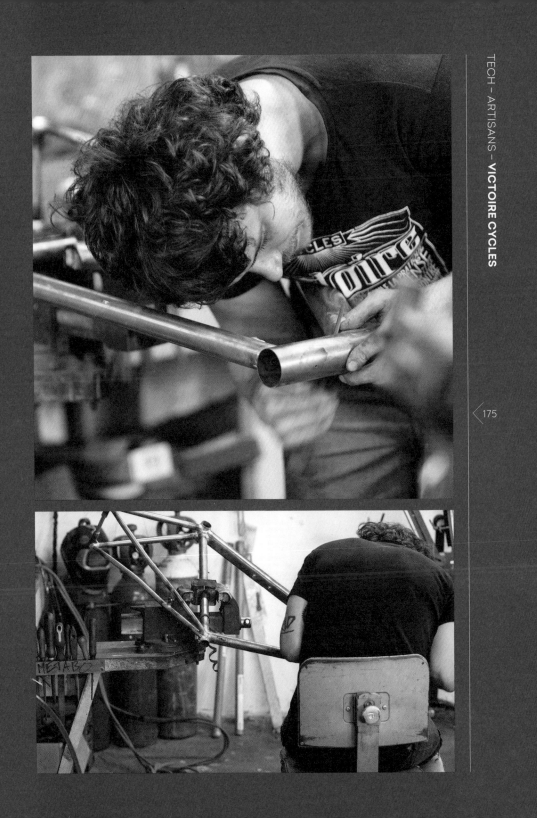

QUENTIN

PROFESSION
Frame-builder

MAKE
ADV

INFO

A true bike lover, Quentin runs his own bike shop – ADV. He knew that, to deepen his knowledge and achieve his goals, he needed to specialize in building steel bicycle frames, and he produced his first custom frame, branded ADV, in 2014.

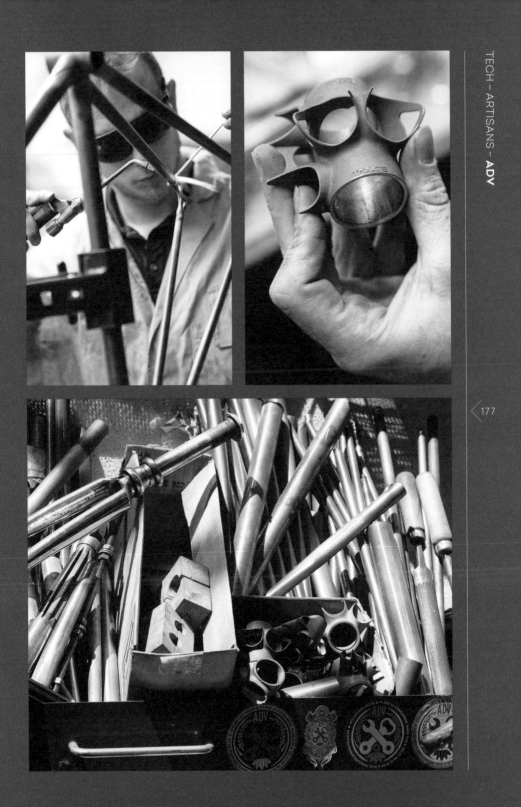

MAXIME

PROFESSION
Frame-builder

MAKE
Belleville Machine

INFO

This former cycle messenger has devoted his life to his passion for bikes. As a teenager, he spent most of his free time – when he wasn't riding his mountain or BMX bikes – tinkering with his machines. He founded Belleville Machine and built his first frames for his messenger colleagues. The quality of Belleville Machine frames made a name for itself, thanks especially to the victory of the Swiss messenger nicknamed "Raph" at the 2014 Cycle Messenger World Championships in Mexico.

PROFESSION
Co-founder of the
Héritage brand

MAKE
Héritage

INFO

A lover of beautiful bicycles, Cyril Saulnier founded the Héritage brand with his associates in response to the destruction of identity and craftsmanship by globalization. In order to meet growing demand for custom bikes, especially from the fixed-wheel fraternity, they attracted the best artisans, including the celebrated frame-builder Daniel Hanart, to offer unique, luxury, high-end bikes.

CHOOSING A FRAME

THE FIRST THING TO CONSIDER WHEN EMBARKING ON A CONVERSION PROJECT IS TO FIND THE BASE – THAT IS, THE BIKE ON WHICH YOU WILL WORK, WHOSE FRAME WILL GENERALLY BE RETAINED. THE FRAME IS ONE OF THE MOST IMPORTANT ELEMENTS OF A BIKE. IT LARGELY DICTATES ITS STYLE, WEIGHT, AND GEOMETRY. WHEN IT IS NOT POSSIBLE TO RESCUE AN OLD BIKE, THESE THREE CRITERIA WILL ENABLE YOU TO CHOOSE THE RIGHT FRAME.

1 – STYLE

This is a matter of personal taste. However, it is possible to repaint a frame to make it look completely different, and to fix any marks or imperfections that the original paintwork may have suffered over time. Repainting a frame is not a difficult process, but it is very time-consuming.

2 – WEIGHT

This might appear unimportant in a conversion project. However, it should be borne in mind that a light bike will demand less effort and thus be more enjoyable to ride, especially up hills. If the frame is a steel one, you should be aware that there are many grades of steel, and that the frame's weight, and often its price, will depend on the grade of steel from which it is made. You can tell which grade by looking at the decal on the frame. Major brands include Columbus, Reynolds, and Vitus.

You may also come across an old aluminium or carbon frame. You should be aware that these materials, though often lighter than steel, tend to age less well. Aluminium can become soft and deformed, while carbon can break suddenly or crack.

Examples of decals giving the name of the frame tubing

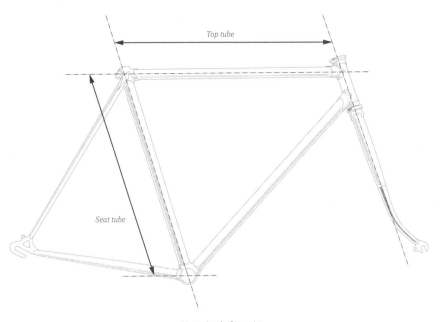

Top tube

Seat tube

Measuring the frame size

3 – GEOMETRY

Several criteria need to be taken into account with regard to the frame's geometry. First, make sure it is the right size for you. Size is generally given as the length of the seat tube, and it can be measured from the centre of the bottom bracket to the seat clamp. The size must be chosen according to your inside leg measurement – from the sole of the foot to the crotch. Since you are most certainly going to use a road

frame as your starting point, it is very important to look at its rear fork ends. For, since fixies and single-speed bikes have no rear derailleur to tension the chain, the only way to do this is to move the rear wheel backwards and forwards within the fork ends. So-called "vertical" fork-ends (road dropouts) do not allow this, so with these, unless you had new fork ends brazed on your frame, you would have to install a chain tensioner, which would spoil the clean lines desired on this type of bike.

The ideal frame for a fixed-wheel bike is a track frame, which has horizontal fork-ends – but in this case we are no longer talking about a conversion.

HEIGHT OF CYCLIST	INSIDE LEG	FRAME SIZE
1.52–1.60m	68–73cm	48 cm
1.61–1.62m	74 cm	48 cm
1.63–1.64m	75 cm	50 cm
1.65–1.66m	76 cm	52 cm
1.67–1.68m	77 cm	52 cm
1.69–1.70m	79 cm	53 cm
1.71–1.74m	81 cm	53 cm
1.75–1.78m	82 cm	54 cm
1.79–1.80m	84 cm	54 cm
1.81–1.82m	86 cm	56 cm
1.83–1.86m	88 cm	56 cm
1.87–1.88m	90 cm	58 cm
1.89–1.92m	91 cm	60 cm
1.92–2.00m	94 cm	60 cm

Choosing the frame size

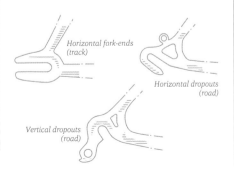

Horizontal fork-ends (track)

Horizontal dropouts (road)

Vertical dropouts (road)

COMPONENTS TO BE RETAINED

ALTHOUGH CONVERSION OF A ROAD BIKE INTO A FIXIE INVOLVES REMOVING CERTAIN COMPONENTS, APART FROM THE FRAME THERE ARE SOME YOU CAN RETAIN.

❶ COCKPIT AND STEERING

The cockpit (handlebar and stem) and steering (fork and headset) can be kept in their entirety although you can choose a different type of handlebar to suit your purposes.

Check that the headset – the two bearings within which the fork rotates in the frame – turns easily and smoothly. Vertical or horizontal play in a headset that is tightened properly is often a sign that it has been damaged, and needs replacing.

It is also common to replace road brake levers with smaller ones more in keeping with the urban style.

❷ BRAKES

On a fixie, there is no point retaining the rear brake, as the pedals will perform the same function. You need only keep the front brake. However, a bit of servicing is essential. Check that the brake isn't rusted, and that the calipers close properly and easily. Replace the brake blocks if they are worn. You can source new brake blocks for any type of caliper without too much difficulty.

❸ SADDLE AND SEATPOST

These, too, can be retained. Since the saddle is the component that most influences comfort on a bike, it should preferably be in good condition, or you risk pain in the buttocks after each ride. The seatpost can be replaced if, for example, it is too rusty. But beware – certain brands, such as Peugeot for instance, used to use seatposts with different diameters from those in use today. So, make sure you check before thinking of getting rid of an old seatpost.

④ WHEELS

These can be retained. However, the rear hub needs to be adapted – or, better, replaced – so that it can be safely fitted with a fixed sprocket. A flip-flop hub, on which you can fit a sprocket on each side, is a good choice for versatility, because it can be fitted with sprockets of different sizes, or a fixed sprocket and a freewheel, making it easy switch from riding fixed to single speed.

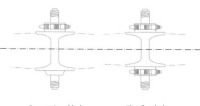

Conventional hub   *Flip-flop hub*

Replacing a hub is no easy task, for wheel-building is a professional job. It is often cheaper to replace the whole wheel than just the hub.

GROUPSET

This is the thorny problem in a conversion, because it is the chief difference between a bike with gears and a fixed-wheel machine. A groupset consists of the bottom bracket, chainset – itself made up of a chainring, or chainrings, and cranks – gear levers, front derailleur, rear derailleur, and a cassette containing a number of sprockets.

⑤ Chainset

A road bike traditionally has two or three chainrings, whereas a fixie needs just one. If you can remove the superfluous chainrings, you won't need to change the chainset unless you want to change the size of a chainring or want cranks of a different length. Indeed, since on a track bike the cranks are always turning, they are shorter than on a road bike, to avoid them catching the ground on tight corners and causing a fall.

The bottom bracket needs careful consideration. There are many different types on the market, and it is best to check your model's compatibility or to seek professional advice.

⑥ Derailleurs and gear levers

These can all be safely removed as they have no function on a fixie.

⑦ Cassette

This, too, needs to be removed and replaced by a fixed sprocket or single freewheel.

⑧ Chain

Even though you can keep your chain by removing some links, it is better to choose a special fixed-wheel chain, which will better withstand wear from continuous pedalling. The chain on a fixie also needs replacing every three years. There are chains specially designed for fixies, known as "half-link" chains, whose length can be adjusted more finely than that of a conventional chain. This is extremely useful if the frame's fork-ends are not specifically designed to take a fixed wheel.

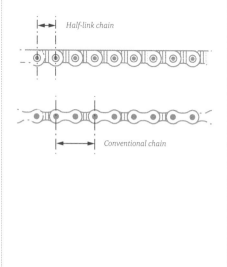

Half-link chain

Conventional chain

CHOOSING REPLACEMENT COMPONENTS

Again, our goal here isn't to teach you how to become a professional mechanic. For this, there are several excellent books, listed at the end of this one. Our goal is rather to help you foresee certain problems you may encounter.

Of these, the issue of different standards is undoubtedly the one that will give you the most headaches. It is worth remembering that bike dimensions are not standard from one country, or generation, to another. So there is no guarantee that an Italian component from the 1970s will be interchangeable with its Japanese or French equivalents from the same era. In fact, there are several historical standards. If your frame is French, it will have been built to French standards that have now fallen out of use. If it is from the United States, Japan, the UK, Germany, or Taiwan, it will certainly have been built to the ISO/BSC standard, which uses inches. If your frame is Chinese or very cheap, it is very likely to have been built to the JIS standard. Finally, if it's from Italy, it will have been built either to Italian standards or, if it is recent, to ISO/BSC ones. All this really is a minefield.

It is therefore advisable, wherever possible, to retain as many components as you can from the original bike. If, for one reason or another, you need to replace a component, the safest solution is to find a used component that is very similar, or a modern copy, which some manufacturers now offer. This applies, for example, to certain components, such as brake calipers, the seatpost, stem, and pedals. If you want to take chances, arm yourself with a caliper and check that the size of the component you want to buy matches that of your frame. That said, in a conversion project there are certain components that must be replaced in order to convert a drivetrain with gears to one with a fixed sprocket.

A NEW HUB FOR YOUR FIXED SPROCKET

Top of the list is, of course, the fixed sprocket. This needs to be fitted to a suitable hub, which will hold the sprocket firmly and line it up correctly with the chainset. As mentioned above, it is simplest to buy a pair of track wheels, because then you won't need to change the hub or rebuild the rear wheel. Many manufacturers now offer wheels for a fixed sprocket suitable for city use, but you can also find used ones for sale privately. In the latter case, check that the wheels are not buckled and haven't suffered an impact.

Another important detail is that track wheels do not have a quick release, but are bolted to the frame. This allows the wheel – which is subject to more stresses on a fixed-wheel machine – to be attached firmly. Although this is not the quickest setup in the event of a puncture, it makes stealing the wheel more problematic...

NEW CHAINSET – NEW BOTTOM BRACKET

Whereas on a road bike it is the rear derailleur that keeps the chain taut and lined up with the sprockets, with a fixed-wheel system it is important to ensure that the sprocket is properly lined up with the chainset. If it isn't, you risk shortening the life of your components, the chain coming off, or, worse, crashing. So, if you establish that your sprocket and chainset are poorly aligned, you should consider re-aligning the chainset. A bike shop specializing in this kind of conversion will, at reasonable cost, replace your period bottom bracket with a modern, sealed unit, usually by re-threading the outdated bottom bracket shell with a current ISO/BSC thread.

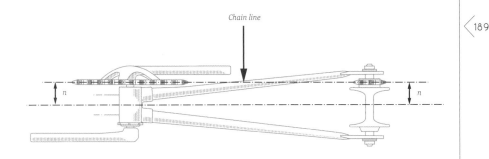

Chain line

NEW CRANKS TO AVOID GROUNDING ON CORNERS

With a fixed-wheel bike, the cranks never stop turning, and it can happen that, when leaning over while cornering, a pedal touches the ground. To avoid this situation, which can lead to a crash, it is best to choose shorter cranks – 165mm being the usual length for a fixie.

A NEW CHAIN TO WITHSTAND THE PRESSURE

As mentioned above, it is best not to skimp on getting a new chain. You can buy tougher chains, designed for track bikes – for the chain must absorb not only the force of acceleration, but also that of braking. If your frame's fork-ends are not long enough to allow the chain tension to be adjusted, you can resort to a "half-link" chain that, thanks to its design of interlocking V-shaped links, allows its length to be adjusted by the equivalent of half a link at a time. This usually means you don't need to use a clunky chain tensioner.

CONCLUSION

You're ready to roll. Just choose your gear and swing into action!

USEFUL INFO

DIARY DATES

CITY CRITERIUMS

Red Hook Crit
Brooklyn, USA – April
London, UK – July
Barcelona, Spain – September
Milan, Italy – October
redhookcrit.com

Rad Race
Berlin, Germany – March
Berlin, Germany – May
Cologne, Germany – June
Rotterdam, Netherlands – July
Heidbergring, Germany
– August
Hamburg, Germany – August
Frankfurt, Germany – August
rad-race.com

National Moutarde Crit
Dijon, France – September
nationalmoutardecrit.com

Bordeaux Critérium Jovial
Bordeaux, France – late July

**Jupiter London Nocturne
City Criterium**
London, UK – June
londonnocturne.com

Kantoikrit
Oñati, Spain – July
kantoikrit.com

Criterium Gijón
Gijón, Spain – August
criteriumgijon.com

RETRO RIDES

Anjou Vélo Vintage
Saumur, France – mid-June
anjou-velo-vintage.com

La Patrimoine
Favières-en-Brie, France
– mid-September
lapatrimoine.fr

Le Ride Béret Baguette
Paris, France – early June
beret-baguette.fr

The Tweed Run
London, UK – April
tweedrun.com

Eroica
Tuscany, Italy – early October
eroicagaiole.com

OTHERS

Festival Vélo en fête
L'Isle-Jourdain, France – June
veloscope.fr

Festival Roulez Jeunesse
**Vélodrome du Parc de la Tête
d'Or, Lyon, France** – early July
roulez-jeunesse.com/festival

Berlin Bicycle Week
Berlin, Germany – March
berlinbicycleweek.com

RESOURCES
BOOKS

Bike Snob
Eben Weiss
(Hardie Grant Books)

New York Bike Style
Sam Polcer & Casey Neistat
(Prestel)

The Bicycle Artisans
Will Jones
(Thames & Hudson Ltd)

*One Gear: Converting
and maintaining single speed
& Fixed gear bicycles*
Matteo Cossu
(Gingko Press, Inc)

*Fixed: Global Fixed-Gear
Bike Culture*
Andrew Edwards &
Max Leonard
(Laurence King Publishers)

WEBZINES

Cycle Exif
cycleexif.com

Manual for speed
manualforspeed.com

No life like this life
nolifelikethislife.com

Copenhagen Cycle Chic
copenhagencyclechic.com

Paris Chill Racing
parischillracing.com

ACKNOWLEDGEMENTS

THANKS TO:

Bénédicte Beaujouan and Nicolas Brulez, without whom this book would probably never have seen the light of day; Suzanne Thoma and Nathalie Floret of the Bureau des Affaires Graphiques, as well as Anne Kalicky of the editorial department, for their high-quality work and for having had faith in me throughout this project, despite problems and delays.

My parents, for having put up with this umpteenth craze; my brother, with whom I often share my passions; my grandmother, whose words, when she heard about this project, deeply touched me; my grandfather, to whom I am indebted for the frame of my conversion bike, and no doubt also for the fantasy bikes going round in my head.

My friends, for their support, and especially Malo for all his help; Yannis for having been behind several of the portraits that appear in this book; Bérangère and Mylène for their invaluable advice; Paul, Simon, Caroline, and Damien for their help in editing several sections; my office colleagues for having put up with all these bikes during the preparation of this book, and especially Domnine, and her help when it got difficult.

My mates at Paris Chill Racing, Pils Bikes Tourism, Paris Bike Polo, the Ride du Mercredi, Surplace, and Steet Pistard...

The whole team at the Bicycle Store and La Crémerie BMX Store, for their invaluable help.

Enzo and Stefano of La Bicyclette.

The Rad Race and Cycles Get Lost teams for their legendary welcomes.

Sylvie, of the French Cycling Federation, and Anthony at the Vélodrome Nation, for allowing me to get close to the champions. And also, all those who have not made it into this book.

An Hachette UK Company
www.hachette.co.uk

First published in Great Britain in 2016
by Mitchell Beazley, a division of
Octopus Publishing Group Ltd
Carmelite House
50 Victoria Embankment
London EC4Y 0DZ
www.octopusbooks.co.uk

Originally published in the French language
under the title *Vélos urbains* © Tana Éditions,
an imprint of Edi8, 12 avenue d'Italie, 75013
Paris, France, 2015

English language translation copyright
© Octopus Publishing Group Ltd 2016

Distributed in the US by
Hachette Book Group
1290 Avenue of the Americas
4th and 5th Floors
New York, NY 10020

Distributed in Canada by
Canadian Manda Group
664 Annette St., Toronto,
Ontario, Canada M6S 2C8

All rights reserved. No part of this work may be
reproduced or utilized in any form or by any
means, electronic or mechanical, including
photocopying, recording or by any information
storage and retrieval system, without the prior
written permission of the publisher.

Laurent Belando asserts the moral right to be
identified as the author of this work.

ISBN 978-1-78472-227-2

A CIP catalogue record for this book is
available from the British Library.

Printed and bound in China.

10 9 8 7 6 5 4 3 2 1

CREDITS

FRENCH EDITION
Produced by Suzanne Thoma of the
Bureau des Affaires Graphiques
www.le-bureau-desaffaires-graphiques.com
Assistant graphic designer Nathalie Floret
Editorial co-ordination and production
Anne Kalicky (Editorial)

ENGLISH EDITION
Commissioning Editor Joe Cottington
Senior Editor Leanne Bryan
Art Director Yasia Williams-Leedham
Typesetter Naomi Edmondson
Production Controller Sarah Kramer